Dictionary of Collective Nouns and Group Terms

A Dictionary of Collective Nouns and Group Terms

Ivan G. Sparkes

Gale Research Company
Book Tower
Detroit, Michigan 48226

First published in the U.S.A.
by Gale Research Company, 1975

ISBN 0 8103 2016 9

Library of Congress Catalog Card
Number 75-4117

Made and printed in Great Britain
for White Lion Publishers Limited,
138 Park Lane, London W1Y 3DD
by Hendington Limited,
Deadbrook Lane, Aldershot, Hampshire

Introduction

Group terms have been in constant use since medieval times, and much of their richness is derived from the language of the chase in use among the knights and esquires of that day. When Sir Arthur Conan Doyle wrote his historical novel entitled 'Sir Nigel' he put into the mouth of an old knight these words of advice . . . 'But above all, I pray you Nigel to have a care in the use of terms of the craft, lest you should make some blunders at table.'

The terms we use today come mainly from those days, and carry a lingering quaintness in their turn of phrase. Many are culled from a rich medieval treasury of hunting terms called 'The Boke of St. Albans' which was compiled by Dame Juliana Berners and printed in 1486. There, in their gothic script, are listed the words in common use and their proper value propounded. Dame Juliana is most anxious that the correct term is found, adding that this is a point which distinguishes the 'gentylman from the ungentylman'. Some of these terms were straightforward words in use for many years, others, I suspect, were somewhat critical comments which reflect the view of medieval man. We may accept the poetic truth in a 'descent of woodpeckers' or a 'watch of nightingales' so I imagine there is equal truth in the rather bitter 'an abomination of monks' referring to that large body of clergy who roamed the countryside from monastery to monastery claiming the benefit of the clergy whenever trouble raised its ugly head.

Since those days we find that their use has diminished until at present they appear lost in the mists of time, practised only in the prose of authors and journalists. Yet they are often colourful and add considerably to the descriptive power of the English language.

During the past century a handful of slim volumes have fortunately recorded new phrases and faithfully reprinted the old, but until now, no systematic dictionary of these terms has been compiled. The words themselves fall into several groups:

(a) Ancient phrases such as 'an exaltation of larks' or 'an abomination of monks' which also reflect some of the views of the medieval users.

(b) General terms such as flock, pile, heap, herd or shoal, which can apply to a wide variety of persons, animals or objects.

(c) Words or names which are made collective by the addition of an ending such as -y or -age; for example, froggery, fruitery, assemblage or brigandage.

(d) Terms which, through misuse or some quirk of change in terminology, relate to one particular group, for instance 'a charm of goldfinches' arises from the archaic 'chirm' (i.e. a din or chatter).

(e) Modern punning terms such as a 'dilation of pupils' and apocryphical comments made in Oxford on seeing a group of prostitutes 'a flourish of strumpets'; a 'jam of tarts' or the more subtle 'anthology of pros'.

(f) Finally are included several terms of quantity, number or capacity which seemed of interest to the compiler.

There is a tendancy nowadays for the punning phrase, especially an alliterative one, to be composed and used in articles or in smart collection of group terms which appear from time to time in the glossy magazines. These are usually passing fancies, and have not the determination to survive found in the older terms. Occasionally a poetic phrase will find favour and by constant repeating implant itself more firmly on the memory, this is what has happened with a 'host of golden daffodils' or the 'monstrous regiment of women'.

In compiling this dictionary, I found my personal knowledge of words was stretched to the limit, and that as others read the proofs they were able to contribute other uses of terms which I had completely overlooked. So I feel that you the reader will suddenly spot an omission, or see an extra use of a group term not listed to date, so do not hesitate to send suggestions for inclusion in any future edition.

For those fascinated in the original medieval terminology, I would recommend recourse to Dame Juliana's 'Boke of St Albans' reprinted in 1881. To those wishing to pursue the etymology of the collective noun, then James Lipton's 'An exaltation of Larks' (1970) will increase your interest. But to those who seek to find the right term to use at the right time, or who are caught in the middle of an intricate crossword puzzle, I dedicate this volume, hoping that one day I might qualify to join a 'labour of lexicographers' or maybe even achieve my ambition by claiming inclusion in a happy 'consort of authors'.

List of published sources

Adams, J. D. The magic and mystery of words. 1963.
Berners, *Dame* Juliana. Boke of St Albans. 1486, facsim. edition 1881.
Book of the British Countryside. 1973.
Doyle, Conan. Sir Nigel. 1906.
Gepp, Edward. An Essex dialect dictionary. 1923, facsim. ed. 1969.
Goss, Helen & Philip. Gathered together. 1928.
Hare, C. E. The language of field sports. 1939, rev. ed. 1949.
Lipton, James. An exaltation of larks. 1970.
Lydgate, John. A lytell treatye of the horse, the sheep and the ghoos. 1499, reprint C.U.P. 1906.
Lynch, S. Group terms of the chase. Chambers Journal.
Oxford English Dictionary on Historical Principles.
Strutt, J. The sports and pastimes of the people of England. 1835 edition.
Webster's New International Dictionary. 1926 edition.
Woodford, M. H. A manual of falconry. 1960.

Part 1

Dictionary of Group Terms and Collective Nouns

ABOMINABLE sight of monks (15th century)

ABUNDANCE (a profusion, a great plenty, *syn* exuberance, plenteousness)
An abundance of good things; of mercy.

ACADEMY (a society of learned men, a school of teaching, *syn* college, institute)
An academy of fanaticism.

ACCRESCENCE (a quantity formed by continuous growth)
An accrescence of belief.

ACCRETION (the coherance of separate particles to form a solid mass)
An accretion of earth.

ACCUMULATION (to heap up, amass, *syn* collection)
An accumulation of energy; of evils; of fortune; of honours; of ire; of knowledge; of power; of snow; of waters; of wealth; of wrath.

AEON (an indefinite period of time)
Aeons of time.

AERIE (a brood of birds of prey, an eyry or eyrie, *syn* brood, nest)
An aerie of children; of eagles; of hawks; of ravens.

AGGLOMERATE (a collection into a ball, heap or mass, *syn* a cluster)
An agglomerate of volcanic fragments.

AGGLOMERATION (a mass or clump of agglomerate things being gathered together, *syn* conglomerate)
An agglomeration of turrets.

AGGREGATE (a mass, assemblage, e.g. a house is an aggregate of bricks, timber, etc., *syn* combination, compound)

AGGREGATION (a collection of parts of a whole; a natural group or body of human beings)
An aggregation of species.

AIRFLEET (a group of aircraft, *collectively*)

ALLIANCE (a union between families, states or parties, also the persons allied, *syn* association, league)

AMBUSH of widows (modern)

ANTHOLOGY (a collection of flowers, therefore of items culled from literature, *syn* garland, treasury)
An anthology of epigrams; of flowers; of hymns; of poems; of prose; *also* in a punning term, an of anthology pros.

ARCHERY (archers, *collectively*)

ARCHIPELAGO (the Grecian Archipelago—hence any sea or broad sheet of water containing islands, *also* a group of islands)

ARCHIVES (a collection of documents)

ARISTOCRACY (the nobles or chief officials in a state, the privileged class)

ARMADA (an armed force, *syn* fleet, squadron, flotilla)
An armada of aircraft; of ships.

ARMOURY (armour, *collectively*)

ARMY (a collection of men armed for battle, *also* a great number, *syn* force, host, troops, array)
An army of ants; of caterpillars; of arguments; of good words; of martyrs; of misfortunes; of sins; of waiters; of words. *See also* SOLDIERS.

AROMA of bakers (modern)

ARRAY (an orderly collection, an imposing series of things, an imposing group of persons, *syn* display)
An array of attorneys (in court); of cliffs; of facts; of figures (numerals); of soldiers; of teeth.

ASSEMBLAGE (a collection of individuals or things, *syn* assembly, cluster)
An assemblage of grace; of ideas; of skaters.

ASSEMBLY (a company of persons collected together at one place, a legislative body, *syn* bevy, company, diet, gathering, group)

ASSOCIATION (a group of persons to promote some idea, sport or object, *syn* alliance, league, fellowship)

ASSORTMENT (a group of things, *syn* miscellany)

AUDIENCE (a group or assembly of listeners, viewers, *also* a formal interview with a person of importance)
An audience of readers.

AUDITORY (an assemblage of listeners and spectators, *syn* audience)

AVENUE (a double row of trees, pillars acting as a passage-way, also used figuratively, *syn* Mall)
Avenue of thoughts; avenues of research.

AVIARY (an enclosure for live birds, hence the birds themselves)

BABBLE of barbers (modern)

BABEL (a confused mixture of sounds, voices or languages, *syn* charivari)

BACHELRY (a group of bachelors; young knights as a class)

BADELYNG of ducks (15th century)

BAG (a varying measure—being the amount contained in a bag of a specified commodity, e.g. 75 kilos of sugar are a bag in Brazil, *also* a game bag and the game it contains)
A bag of tricks.

BAL (a collection of mines, *Cornish*)

BALE (a large bundle or collection, usually round in shape, *also* a set of dice)

BALK (a ridge or heap, *syn* bank or bar)
A balk of earth; of sand.

BALUSTRADE (a row of balusters)

BALL (a round or roundish body or mass, *syn* orb, globe, clew)
Ball of fire; of twine.

BAND (a company of persons, sometimes of animals, a company of musicians, *syn* company)
A band of followers; of fugitives; of gorillas (a male with one or more females and young); of musicians; of outlaws; of pilgrims; of plovers; of robbers; of strangers.

BANDITTI (a company of bandits)

BANK (a mound, pile or ridge, a group or series of objects, *syn* balk, bar, bench)
A bank of clouds; of electric lights; of judges (a full court in which the judges are 'in bank'); of organ keys; of sand; of snow; of swans.

BANNER (a body of men or troops who follow a banner, a group of knights)

BAR (a band of sand or gravel, especially at the mouth of a river, *also* barristers or lawyers, *collectively*)

BAREN (a pack or herd of mules, taken from barren, i.e. not capable of producing young)

BARONAGE *or* **BARONEY** (the whole body of barons)

BARRING (bars, *collectively*, i.e. decorative bars or stripes)

BASINFUL of trouble (a load of worries)

BASK of crocodiles.

BATCH (a group or collection of persons or things of the same kind, or taken or made at the same time, *syn* sort or lot)
A batch of bread (the quantity baked at one time); of letters; of notes; of politics; of visitors.

BATTALION (the main body of an army, an infantry command of two or more companies forming part of a regiment)

BATTERY (a number of similar machines or devices arranged in a group, *also* a succession of blows or drum beats; a number of birds housed together to encourage the laying of eggs, *syn* bank, bench)
A battery of boilers; of condensers; of dynamos; of electric lights; of guns (i.e. a gun battery or emplacement); of hens; of kitchen utensils; of leyden jars; of lights; of prisms or lens; of searchlights.

BAVIN (a bundle of brushwood, *syn* tuft, tassel)

BAYONET (a group of soldiers armed with bayonets)

BEACH (pebbles *or* sand, *collectively*)

BEACONAGE (a system of beacons)

BEAM (a ray or collection of parallel rays, *syn* ray)
Beam of heat; of light rays; of sunlight.

BEAT (a quantity to be beaten or processed at once; a bundle of flax or hemp made up ready for steeping)

BED (a layer or bed-like mass, small animals, especially reptiles grouped together, *syn* layer)
A bed of ashes; of clams; of coal; of cockles; of eels; of mussels; of oysters; of snakes; of scorpions; of worms.

BELLOWING of bullfinches.

BEGGARY (beggars, *collectively*)

BELT (a continuous series of objects usually encircling something, a broad strip of any kind)
A belt of ice; of paternosters; of trees.

BELTING (belts, *collectively*)

BENCH (officials, *collectively*; judges, *collectively*; something likened to a bench, *syn* bank)
A bench of aldermen; of bishops; of judges; of magistrates; of organ keys; of show dogs.

BEVY (a drinking company, an assembly or collection, *syn* flock)
Bevy of beauties; of conies; of fairies; of ladies; of larks; of maids of heaven; of otter; of quail; of renegades; of roes (six head of roe deer); of slaves; of swans.

BEW (a flock of partridge, *syn* bow, flock)

BIBLIOGRAPHY (a collection of book titles arranged in a special order, or relating to a special subject)

BIKE (a swarm or crowd of people, a nest of wild bees etc.) A bike of ants; of hornets; of wasps; of wild bees.

BIND (a unit of measurement for salmon or eels) A bind of eels (ten sticks, i.e. 250 eels); a bind of salmon (fourteen gallons).

BING (a heap or pile, particularly of metallic substances)

BISHOPDOM (bishops, *collectively*)

BITE of mites.

BLACKENING of shoemakers. *See* BLECHE.

BLARNEY of bartenders (modern)

BLAST of hunters (15th century, pun on the blast of the hunter's horn)

BLECHE of sowters (15th century, this has been translated as a blackening of shoemakers)

BLOAT of hippotami (modern)

BLOCK (a quantity, number or a section of something) A block of bonds or shares; of flats.

BLOW (a quantity of steel dealt with at one time in a Bessemer converter)

BLUSH of boys (15th century, pun on the shyness of adolescent boys)

BOARD (a council convened for business, a number of persons appointed or elected to sit on a committee) Board of directors; of guardians.

BOAST of soldiers (15th century, pun on exploits recounted by returning soldiers)

BOATERY (boats, *collectively*)

BODY (a number of individuals spoken of collectively; a general collection of things or ideas; a mass of matter)
A body of cold air; of divinity, facts, laws; of horse; of light; of opinion; of scriptures; of troops.

BOLL (measure of capacity for grain, six bushels in Scotland, *also* measure of weight, 140 lb)

BOLT (a bundle, a compact packet, a roll of woven fabric)
A bolt of canvas (40 yds); of cloth (40 yds); of glass (a molten cylindrical jet); osiers (willow twigs); of silk (40 yds); of straw; of water (a cylindrical jet).

BOOK (collection of tablets, sheets of paper or similar material strung or bound together)
A book of gold leaf; of silk (a bundle of skeins of raw silk).

BOOLY (a company of herdsmen wandering to find pasture with their cattle)

BOOM (a fixed line of floating timber)

BOREDOM (bores, *collectively*)
Boredom of briefs (modern)

BOSK (bosquet, bosket or boscage, a grove or plantation of shrubs or trees)

BOTTLE (a bundle of hay or straw)

BOUQUET (a nosegay or bunch, cluster etc., *syn* bow or bough pot)
A bouquet of feathers; of fireworks (a large flight of rockets); of flowers; of herbs; of pheasants (the flight of a flock from the beaters); of rockets; of trees.

BOUROCK (a stone heap, mound, confused heap)

BOW (a herd of cattle, *also* the cattle on a farm)

BOW *or* **BOUGHPOT** (a bouquet of flowers or boughs)

BOYHOOD (boys, *collectively*)

BRACE (a pair; a couple, originally of dogs, rarely used for people, *syn* cast (i.e. set))
A brace of bishops; of bucks; of ducks; of foxes; of greyhounds; of hares; of hounds; of orthopaedists (modern pun); of partridges; of pheasants; of pike; of pistols; of trout.

BRACKETING (brackets, *collectively*)

BRANCHING (a collection of branches)

BRASH (a mass of fragments or debris, *also* a sudden outburst of rain)
A brash of hedge clippings; of ice; of rain.

BREAK (a large quantity, a lot or consignment, a great number)
A break of tea.

BREED (a race or variety of animals, a class, a sort, a kind of men, things or qualities, *also* a number produced at one time, *syn* a brood)
A breed of thinkers; of wits.

BREWING (a collection of black clouds which signal a storm)

BRIGADE (a company or band of people, a body of troops, any body of persons acting together for a purpose, e.g. Fire Brigade)
A brigade of papists; of trappers.

BRIGANDAGE (brigands or robbers, *collectively*)

BROOD (the young of animals, the young of bird, hatched or reared at the same time or from the same dam, *syn* aerie, fry, breed)
Brood of chicken; of daughters; of eagles; of eggs; of folly; of grouse; of guilty wishes; of hawks; of hens; of kittens; of lies; of small boats.

BROTHERHOOD (an association, or guild, a profession, persons or things of like kind or interests, *syn* fraternity, fellowship)

BRUSH (a bundle of light rays—usually of weak intensity)

BUDGET (a bag or sack with its contents, a stock or accumulation, *also* an estimate of expenses)
A budget of inventions; of paradoxes; of news.

BUILDING (a flock of rooks, *syn* rookery)

BULK (the main mass or amount, a heap or cargo, a considerable amount, *syn* volume, mass)
A bulk of popery; of ships; of tobacco (a pile arranged for curing)

BULLARY (a collection of Papal bulls or documents)

BUNCH (a cluster or tuft, properly of things of one type growing or fastened together, *also* a group of things or animals of the same type close together, *syn* bundle, nosegay)
A bunch of bananas; of cattle; of cherubs; of ducks; of fives (a clenched fist); of grapes; of keys; of linen yarn (60 hanks); of patriarchs; of prophets; of tunes; of vapours; of waterfowl; of widgeon.

BUNDLE (a number of things bound together such as a loose package or roll, a given quantity of some article, *syn* a bolt, bunch, package, collection)
A bundle of archdeacons; of calumnies; of linen yarn (20 hanks); of notes (money); of papers; of paper (2 reams); of qualities; of rays; of sensations; of sticks; of straw; of superstitions.

BURDEN (a fixed quantity of a commodity, *syn* load, charge, trust)
A burden of sin; of steel (120 pounds); of sorrows.

BUREAUCRACY (government officials, *collectively*)

BURST (a vehement outburst, *syn* round)
A burst of applause; of passion; of thunder.

BURY of conies (a burrow *or* rabbits, *collectively*)

BUSH (bushes, *collectively*, a cluster of shrubs; a bush-like mass such as of foliage or feathers, woodland or rural countryside, *collectively* as opposed to the town, *syn* brush)
A bush of ivy (a branch of ivy hung as a vintner's sign); of thorns.

BUSINESS of flies (flies, *collectively*)

BUSYNESS of ferrets (ferrets, *collectively*)

BUZZ of barflies (modern)

CABAL (a small group engaged in a secret intrigue, *syn* faction, camarilla, conspiracy)
A cabal of artists; of intriguers; of politicians (its use was popular relating to the period of 1670 when the Government Ministers included Clifford, Ashley, Buckingham, Arlington and Lauderdale)

CABIRI (a group of deities of Samothrace)

CABOODLE (the whole amount, the lot)

CACHE (a hiding place, *also* that which is hidden)
A cache of jewels; of provisions; of treasure.

CADE (a cask or barrel containing a quantity of 720 herrings)

CADRE (a group or skeleton of trained men who would absorb untrained men to form an efficient unit)

CAIRN (a pile of stones, usually erected to mark a spot as a memorial)

CAKE (a mass of matter moulded into a solid shape)
A cake of dynamite; of ice; of paint; of soap; of tobacco; of wax.

CALENDAR (an orderly list of persons things or events)
A calendar of academics; of documents; of saints.

CALLING (a group of persons following a profession, in particular the Church)

CAMARILLA (a company of secret or irresponsible councillors, for example the King's circle of advisers, *syn* cabal, coterie, clique)

CAMP (a collection of tents, the company or body of people who are encamped, a great number, a body of people joined to promote some theory or doctrine, *syn* host)
A camp of allegations; of arguments; of facts; potatoes (a ridge-shaped heap); turnips (a ridge-shaped heap)

CANAILLE (the rabble, mob, the lowest class of people, *syn* rabble)

CANNONRY (cannons, *collectively* (military use))

CANON (collection of rules, laws, set of mathematical tables, *syn* code)
Canon of monastic rules; of saints.

CANOPY (an overhanging shelter or shade, *also* used figuratively)
A canopy of clouds; of trees.

CANTEEN (a chest or case for carrying culinary utensils, hence a collection of the items themselves)
A canteen of cutlery.

CANVAS (paintings, *collectively*; sails, *collectively*; tents, *collectively*)

CAPFUL of wind

CARAVAN (a number of people travelling together; a moving company, a fleet of merchant ships (rare), *syn* convoy)
A caravan of camels; of merchants; of pilgrims; of travellers.

CARDINALATE (cardinals, *collectively*)

CARNAGE (carcasses, *collectively*)

CAROL (a band or company, a circle or ring of things, a ring dance with songs, therefore the songs themselves, *syn* choir)
A carol (singers, *collectively*): a carol of maidens; a carol of standing stones; a carol of virgins.

CARROT (a group of objects which form the shape of a carrot)
A carrot of tobacco.

CARTLOAD (a large and mixed quantity)
A cartload of complaints; of grievances; of lies; of monkeys (*from* artful as a cartload of monkeys)

CASCADE (something suggestive of a fall of water, *syn* spray)
A cascade of fireworks; of jewels; of lace; of rockets; of volcanic ashes.

CASE (set or pair, a box and its contents; *syn* brace)
A case of coxcombs; of instruments; of pistols; of rapiers; of teeth.

CASKET (something likened to a casket of jewels)
A casket of literary selections; of musical selections.

CAST (the things or quantity thrown or produced at one time; a group of actors in a play, a set or suit of armour, a couple of birds, *syn* set, brood, brace)
Cast of actors; of armour; of bees (an afterswarm); of bread (baked at one time); of falcons; of goshawks; of grain (amount harvested); of hawks (two); of herrings (number thrown into a vessel at one time); of lackeys; of lambs (number born at one time); of oysters; of seed (amount scattered at one time); of vultures (two)

CASTLE (any structure or pile of objects more or less in the shape of a castle)
A castle of cards.

CATALOGUE (a list of names, titles or articles arranged methodically, *syn* calendar)
A catalogue of librarians (punning term); of sins; of virtues.

CATARACT (a violent downpour or rush, anything likened to a cataract, *syn* cascade)
A cataract of nastiness; of panegyrics; of water.

CATCH (the quantity caught or taken at one time, also used figuratively, *syn* cast, bag)
A catch of favourite stories; of fish.

CAUCUS (an inner committee which works behind the back of the main party)

CAVALCADE (a procession of persons on horseback, or of carriages, a company of horsemen in procession or marching)
A cavalcade of horsemen; of songs.

CAVALRY (horses or horsemen, *collectively*)

CAVE (a small group of politicians who secede from the main party on a particular question)

CELL (a small religious group or community connected to a monastery or convent, a unit of persons forming part of a network in a political party—a communist cell)

CELLAR (a place for storing wine, hence the wine bottles, *collectively*)

CELLARAGE (cellars, *collectively*)

CENOBY (a religious community)

CENTEENER (a large number of plants or animals having a common parentage)

CENTO (a literary or musical composition made up of selections, a string or rigmarole)
A cento of blunders; of common-places; of scripture phrases; of verses.

CENTURY (a group of a hundred things)
A century of prayers; of words.

CETE (an assemblage or company)
A cete of badgers; of greys.

CHAIN (a series of things linked together by an actual or figurative chain, *syn* cordon, series)
A chain of buckets; of events; of human beings; of ideas; of islands; of lakes; of mountains; of proof; of reasoning; of shops; of storms; of thoughts.

CHANGE *or* peal of bells.

CHANTRY (a body of priests who say masses for the dead in a chantry chapel)

CHAOS (any confused or disordered collection or state of things, *syn* confusion, clutter)
Chaos of accidental knowledge.

CHAPEL (a choir of singers, an association of journalists, of printers)

CHAPELRY (a congregation of nonconformist chapel-goers)

CHAPLET (a string of beads or a garland, or something which resembles it)
A chaplet of beads; of domestic affections; of flowers; of prayers; of toad's eggs.

CHAPTER (the body or community of an organized branch of a society or church, *also* something which forms a series, as of topics, sections of a book, or periods of one's life)
Chapter of accidents; of canons; of friars; of knights; of noble virgins; of possibilities.

CHARGE (a load, burden or weight, a quantity, as of shot to fill a gun, or of ore to fill a furnace, a mental or moral load, *syn* burden, trust)
A charge of curates (15th century); of gunpowder; of shot.

CHARIOTRY (warriors who fought from chariots, *collectively*)

CHARIVARI (a medley of discordant sounds, *syn* babel)

CHARM of goldfinches (goldfinches, *collectively*) *see also* CHIRM

CHARTULARY (a collection or register of charters, *syn* archives)

CHATTERING of choughs, *also* starlings (*collectively*)

CHAUTAUQUA (an educational assembly, modelled on that at Lake Chautauqua in U.S.A. in 1874)

CHERUBIM – cherubs (*collectively*)

CHEST (a box, also the quantity or things contained, *syn* case)
A chest of tools; of viols.

CHILIAD (a group of 1,000 things)

CHILIARCHY (a body of 1,000 troops)

CHIME (a peal of bells)

CHIRM (a din or chatter, hence its use as a group term for finches) *see also* CHARM

CHOIR (an organised company of persons or things, a company of singers, a band or company of dancers, an order or division of angels, *syn* carol or chorus)
A choir of angels; of choristers; of dancers; of echoes; of muses; of planets; of tents.

CHORUS (a company of singers, simultaneous outburst of speech, *syn* choir, carol)
A chorus of bad language; of Greek actors; of laughter; of planets; of singers.

CHRESTOMATHY (a selection of choice literary passages)

CIRCLE (a set or series of parts connected to form a whole, a company assembled about a central point or topic of interest, a circular ring of persons or things, *syn* ring, circlet, company)
A circle of admirers; of acquaintances; of onlookers; of pleasures; a literary circle.

CITADEL (mole burrows at different levels connected by vertical shafts)

CLAM (a stack or pile of bricks or oysters)

CLAMOUR of rooks (a flock)

CLAN (a social group of common descent, a body of persons with some common interest, a collection of animals, plants or lifeless things, *syn* clique, sept, society)

CLAQUE (a group of admirers always ready to applaud the leader, in France a group of paid applauders)

CLATTER (a mass of loose stones scattered, *syn* Clutter)

CLATTERING of choughs.

CLAUT (a handful, a rakeful, *from* the verb to claw or scratch)

CLERKAGE *or* **CLERKERY** (clerks, *collectively*, probably relates to holy clerks)

CLETCH (alternative of clutch, i.e. a brood or hatching)

CLEW (globe, ball, a round bunch)
A clew of worms; of thread; of yarn or cord.

CLIENTELE (a body of clients, a group of adherents or supporters)

CLIQUE (a narrow circle of friends, an exclusive set, *syn* coterie, faction)
A clique of admirers.

CLOSING of taverners (15th century—a group of inn-keepers)

CLOTHING (clothes, suits, etc., *collectively*)

CLOUD (a mass or volume of smoke, flying dust; a great crowd, a vast collection, *syn* drift)

A cloud of arrows; of flies; of gnats; of grasshoppers; of incense; of information; of locust; of sails; of seafowl; of starlings; of witches; of witnesses.

CLOWDER (kendle or kindle of cats)

CLUMP (an unshaped mass; a heap, *syn* group, thicket)
A clump of houses; of plants; of reeds; of trees.

CLUSTER (a number of like things growing together; a number of similar things collected together, *syn* bunch, crowd)
A cluster of bees; of churls; of churches; of crystals; of grapes; of houses; of icebergs; of islands; of nuts; of spiders; of stars; of woes.

CLUTCH (a nest of eggs or brood of chicks, *syn* family, brood) *see also* CLETCH
A clutch of chicken; of constables; of eggs; of geese; of partridges; of squalls (weather); of tempests.

CLUTTER (confused collection, *syn* clatter)
A clutter of cats; of citations; of consonants; of spiders.

COALITION (union of a mass of separate bodies or parts, an alliance of persons, states or political parties, *syn* league, combination, fusion)

COB (a rounded heap or mass, a bunch of hair, a small stack of grain or hay)

COCK (a conical heap of produce, e.g. hay in the field)

CODE (a collection of laws, rules, signals, a body of writings, *syn* canon)
Code of good manners; of laws; of rules; of scriptures.

CODEX (a collection of recipes for the preparation of drugs)

COHORT (a division in the Roman army, *also* a band of warriors, *syn* company or band)
A cohort of acquaintances; of warriors.

COIL (a series of rings, a spiral, a series of connected pipes in rows or layers)

COLLATION (a collection as of money, *also* of food, *syn* a contribution)
A collation of chicken; of salad.

COLLECTANEA (passages collected from various authors, *syn* a miscellany, anthology)

COLLECTION (a gathering or assemblage of objects or of persons)

COLLECTIVE (a collective body, a gathering, a collection of extracts; in U.S.S.R., a farm created by pooling together a number of small holdings)

COLLEGE (a body of colleagues or students, a collective body, a community of clergy, a society of students, *syn* academy, institute)
A college of bees; of canons; of cardinals; of courtesans; of executioners; of handmaidens; of heralds.

COLLOQUIUM (a conference, a group discussion which takes its name from colloque, a place for conversation in a monastery)

COLLUVIES (a medley, a rabble, usually unpleasant)

COLONY (a group of people transplanted to another province or country, a group of persons engaged in the same occupation, a number of animals or plants living together, *syn* community)
A colony of ants; of artists; of auks (on land); of avocets; of badgers; of bats; of bees; of chinchilla; of cormorants; of frogs; of gulls; of ibises; of lepers; of mice; of voles.

COLUMN (anything resembling a column in form or function, *syn* pillar)
A column of accountants (modern pun); of figures; of infantry (usually on the march); of smoke; of troops.

COMBINATION (union of persons to effect a purpose, a series of letters, incidents, *syn* alliance, coalition)

COMBINE (a group of persons originally combining for a conspiracy or for fraudulent purposes, now usually a very large commercial company)

COMITADJI (a band of irregulars)

COMITATUS (companions, *collectively*, a body of well-born men attached to a king or chieftain by the duty of military service, *see also* POSSE COMITATUS)

COMITIA (an assembly of the people to act on matters presented to them, an assembly)

COMMAND (a military or naval force, a body of troops)

COMMITTEE (a body of persons who are appointed or elected to administer)

COMMIXTURE (a compound, mixture)
A commixture of virtues and vices.

COMMONALTY (the common people, the mass of a corporate body, i.e. the mayor and the commonalty of a city)

COMMONTY (a community, *syn* commonalty)

COMMONWEALTH (a body of persons constituting a state or community, a body united for some interest, *syn* state, realm, republic)
The commonwealth of learning; the British Commonwealth.

COMMUNE (a body forming an interim government, in particular in Paris 1794 and 1871)

COMMUNION (a body of Christians having a common faith and discipline, *syn* fellowship)
Communion of saints; the Anglican Communion, etc.

COMMUNITY (a body of people having a common organization or interest, a common language or nationality)
A community of flies; of monks; of ulcers; *also* European Community.

COMPAGES (a system or union of many parts, *syn* framework)
Compages of pipes and vessels.

COMPAGINATION (a union of parts, a structure)

COMPANY (a fellowship, band, retinue, *syn* assembly, band, bevy)
A company of actors (often used collectively); of apostles; of moles; of musicians; of parrots; of players; of prophets; of ships (a merchant fleet); of soldiers; of widgeon.

COMPLEMENT (the full quantity, a complete set, the personnel on a ship or establishment)

COMPLEX (an assemblage or items made up from a number of intricate parts, frequently used in relation to a group of buildings)
A complex of psychoanalysts (modern pun)

COMPOSITION (an aggregate, mixture of a body formed by combining two or more items)

COMRADERY (comradeship, i.e. a group of comrades)

CONCATENATION (a series or groups dependent on each other or linked in some way, *syn* a chain)
A concatenation of bungles and contradictions; of causes and effects; of explosions; of ideas; of felicity.

CONCENT (a harmony of sounds)

CONCERT (an agreement, harmony or union of things or persons; a combination of sounds or of performers on instruments, a set of instruments)
A concert of angels; of Europe (agreement of power on the Eastern Question); of terrific vociferation.

CONCILIABLE (a small or private assembly, usually of illegal religious groups)

CONCLAVE (a close or secret meeting)
A conclave of cardinals; of teachers; of prelates.

CONCOURSE (a moving crowd of people or things, *syn* assemblage)
A concourse of books; of people (moving together)

CONDESCENSION of actors (modern pun)

CONE (a conical mass, also used figuratively, *syn* cock)

CONE-IN-CONE (a series of parallel cones)

CONFEDERACY (a body of persons, states or nations, a combination of persons to do unlawful acts, *syn* league, alliance, union)

CONFECTION (a composition, a mixture, also used in a musical or literary sense)

CONFESSION (religious body or church, united by a confession of faith, *syn* Communion)

CONFIGURATION (a group of stars)

CONFLUENCE (a crowd, multitude, concourse flocking together, *syn* concourse)
A confluence of associations (historical, etc.); of comforts; of joys; of successes; of visitors.

CONFUSION (a confused collection, *syn* clutter, chaos)
A confusion of blocks of stones; of persons.

CONGERIES (a collection of particles, parts or things, a heap, *syn* aggregation)
Congeries of ballads; of rocks; of stars; of watery particles; of furniture shops.

CONGESTION (a gathering or accumulation, heap or pile)
A congestion of population; of traffic; of tumult.

CONGIARY (a present or largess given in Roman times to soldiers or people, named after a congius which is a measure of three quarts)
A congiary of corn; of oil; of wine.

CONGLOBATION (gathered together into a globule or small globe, *syn* conglomerate)

CONGLOMERATE (gathered into a mass or ball, closely crowded, as of flowers)
A conglomerate of anecdotes; of fragments; of flowers; of useful (or useless) knowledge; of geologists (modern pun)

CONGLOMERATION (a collection, of that which is conglomerated)
A conglomeration of chances; of sounds; of words.

CONGREGATION (an assembly of persons or things; a group of religious persons under a common rule, *also* the Christian Church collectively, *syn* community, confession)
Congregation of apostles; of cardinals; of fine qualities; of goods; of hypocrites; of monasteries (e.g. the Congregation of Cluny); of people; of plovers (a flock); of vapours; of winds.

CONGRESS (a formal assembly of representatives of a trade, a union or some other body)

CONJUGATION (an assembly, being joined together, a combination)
A conjugation of atoms; of miracles; of probabilities.

CONJUNCTION of grammarians (modern pun)

CONJUNCTURE (combination of events or circumstances)
Conjuncture of circumstances; of principles; grand conjuncture (when several planets or stars are found together)

CONNECTION (a religious society, *syn* denomination, sect)

CONSECTION (a series of things which follow each other)

CONSERVATORY (a school of advanced studies, specializing in one of the fine arts, therefore the body of students and professors therein)

CONSISTORY (any solemn assembly or council, *syn* conclave)
Consistory of bishops; of saints; of martyrs; of senators.

CONSORT (a number of people consorting together or in company, a company or set of musicians, *syn* concert)
A consort of authors; of bird calls; of fiddlers; of musicians; of parasites; of ships (sailing together); of viols; of virgins.

CONSORTIA *or* **CONSORTIUM** (partnership, union, fellowship)
A consortium of local authorities; of university libraries; a housing consortia.

CONSTABULARY (constables, *collectively*)

CONSTELLATION (a group of fixed stars, an assembly of great splendour; a group of famous people)
A constellation of genius; of stars.

CONSTERNATION of mothers (modern pun)

CONSULT (a council meeting for consultation; a group meeting for conspiracy or intrigue)
A consult of catholics; of coquettes; of Jesuits.

CONVENT (an association of religious persons secluded from the world; an assembly or meeting; a body of monks, friars or nuns; a company of twelve (or with the Superior, thirteen) monks or nuns (*syn* nunnery, monastery))
Convent of apostles; of merchants; of witches.

CONVENTICLE (a small or private assembly, a meeting for religious worship, *also* a clandestine or irregular meeting, *syn* conciliable)

CONVENTION (a body or assembly, especially a meeting of representatives of some profession, society or religious group, *syn* congress)

CONVERTING of preachers (a company of preachers, 15th century)

CONVOCATION (an assembly of people convoked, i.e. called together, such as the Convocation of Canterbury or of York (a group of high ranking clergy), *also* used in relation to tinners in Cornwall)
Convocation of eagles.

CONVOY (a funeral train or cortège, a party of ships escorting unarmed vessels, a company at a marriage that goes to meet the bride, *syn* caravan)
Convoy of mourners; of ships; of wedding guests.

CORD (a cubic measure 8 feet × 4 feet × 4 feet)
A cord of rock; of stone; of wood.

CORDON (a line or series of people or objects placed at intervals, usually for fortification or attack, *syn* chain)
Cordon of police; of troops.

CORE (a body of individuals, a company which forms the central or main unit of a group, organization or society, *also* players in a curling match, miners in one shift)

CORNET (a troop of cavalry)
A cornet of horse.

CORPS (an organized body of men, usually military, also of students)
A corps of anatomists (modern pun)

CORPUS (a body or collection of writings on a subject, usually the whole literature on the subject; or all the writings of one author)

CORROBOREE (a hilarious or slightly riotous assembly, based on the Australian dance)

CORTÉGE (a procession, a train of attendance, a funeral procession)

COTERIE (a number of people meeting familiarly, usually for social or literary purposes, *syn* set, clique, coterie)
A coterie of orchids.

COUNCIL (an assembly elected or appointed for the government of a state, city or society, *also* used when physicians consult in a serious case)

COURT (the retinue of a sovereign, an organization for administration of justice, a body of directors, managers, delegates, courtiers, *collectively*)

COVEN (a company or assembly, more particularly a covin or convent of witches, *syn* convent, covin)

COVERT (a flock of birds, *syn* covey)
Covert of coots.

COVEY (a flock of birds, a brood or hatch of birds, *syn* covert, company or bevy)
Covey of coxcombs; of doctrines; of fiddlers; of girls; of grouse; of mathematicians; of partridges; of ptarmigans; of victims.

COVIN (a number of persons banded together, *syn* coven)
Covin of heathen; of wicked men; of witches.

COW (a bunch of twigs, a birch or besom)

COWARDICE of curs (15th century)

CRAFT (vessels, *collectively*; a brotherhood of freemasons; those engaged in a craft or trade)

CRAN (a measure of fish, about 750 herrings)

CRASH of rhinoceros (modern pun)

CRATE (a measure of glass, twelve plates on a table, also used loosely to indicate a large amount)

CREAGHT (a herd of cattle driven from place to place for pasture, *syn* bow, booly)

CRÉCHE (a group of infants)

CREDENCE of sewers (15th century, a sewer is a servant in charge of serving the dishes or water for washing the hands of guests at the table)

CREW (a company, squad, gang, *syn* complement)
A crew of airmen; of critics; of gipsies; of pirates; of sailors.

CROCKERY (crocks or china, *collectively*)

CROCODILE (a long line of persons or things)
A crocodile of schoolgirls.

CROP (product or yield of anything growing, or something resembling a crop)
A crop of beardless youths; of crystals; of corn; of goose-pimples; of lies; of petty discussions; of turkeys; of ulcers; of wheat.

CROWD (a number of persons or things closely pressed together, *syn* company, set)
A crowd of advertisements; of islands; of names; of rivals; of sail; of sins; of redwing.

CRUSH (a vast crowd of persons or things)

CRY of players (modern pun, actors, *collectively*); of hounds.

CURSE of painters (painters, *collectively*), *also* a curse of creditors (modern pun)

CUTTING of cobblers (cobblers, *collectively*)

CYCLE (a long indefinite time, set or series)
Cycle of champions; of changes; of epics; of morality; of poems; of seasons; of songs; of sonnets; of years.

DAIRY (milking cows, *collectively*)

DAMNED (the souls in hell)

DAMNING of jurors (the jury, a pun on their power to condemn)

DARG (a specific quantity of work)

DEBACLE (a confused rush or route)
A debacle of water (a violent rush of water)

DEBAUCHING of bachelors (modern pun)

DEBRIS (the remains or anything broken down, ruins, etc., the accumulation of loose material or rock, vegetable or animal matter)

DECADARCHY (a ruling council of ten members)

DECADE (a group or set or series of ten)
A decade of prayers, of soldiers, of years.

DECANTER of deans (deans, *collectively*)

DECEIT of lapwing (a flock)

DECK (a heap or store, a pile of things laid flat upon each other)
A deck of cards.

DECORUM of deans (deans, *collectively*)

DELEGATION (group of persons appointed to represent others)

DELIRIUM of debutantes (modern pun)

DEMOCRACY (the population of a democratic state)

DEN (a wild beasts' lair, hence the beasts themselves)
Den of fox families; of snakes; of thieves; of vice.

DENOMINATION (a society, class or sect of persons called by the same name and of the same views, *syn* confession, communion)
Denomination of Baptists; of Christians; of Methodists.

DEPUTATION (persons or group of persons appointed or deputed to act on behalf of others, *syn* delegation)

DESCENT of woodpeckers.

DESERT of lapwing.

DESTRUCTION of wild cats.

DETACHMENT (that which is detached, a body of troops; part of a fleet, *syn* detail)
A detachment of troops.

DETAIL (a small body of men detailed or detached for special duties, *syn* detachment)

DIET (a formal public assembly, i.e. the Diet of Worms, 1521, *syn* assembly)

DIGEST (a digested collection of statements or information)
A digest of laws.

DIGNITY of canons (15th century, canons, *collectively*)

DILATION of pupils (a modern pun)

DILIGENCE of messengers (15th century, messengers, *collectively*)

DISAGREEMENT of statesmen (modern pun)

DISCRETION of priests (priests, *collectively*)

DISGUISING of tailors (tailors, *collectively*)

DISPLAY (a series of things, a group of persons participating in a gymnastic or military display, *syn* array)

DISSIMULATION of birds (a flock)

DISWORSHIP of Scots (derogatory term)

DIVAN (a collection of sheets, hence a collection of poems, a register of accounts)

DOCTRINE of doctors (doctors, *collectively*, i.e. Ph.D. *not* M.D.)

DOGGERY (dogs, *collectively*)

DOLE (a portion, a share)

DOLE (a company of doves, also dule)

DOLLOP (a large amount)

DOPPING of sheldrakes (a flock)

DOSSIER (a bundle of papers in reference to some matter or relating to a person)

DOUT of wild cats.

DOWN of hares; of sheep.

DOZEN (a collection of twelve objects, *also* an indefinite small number)
A dozen of bread; of wine; of ale; of beer.

DOYLT of swine (swine, *collectively*)

DRAFT *or* **DRAUGHT** (a load, the quantity drawn forward, a chosen detachment of men, *syn* detachment, detail)
A draft of bottlers; of butlers; of cars (used for duty purposes); of cattle (selected or culled from the herd); of eels (20 pounds); of fish; of sailors; of soldiers.

DRAM (a minute quantity; a small draught of cordial or liquor, also used figuratively)
A dram of constancy; of gin; of learning; of mercy; of poison; of well doing.

DRAVE (a haul or shoal of fish)

DRAY of squirrels.

DRIFT (a number of animals driven or moving along in a body; mass of matter driven forward, *syn* drive, creaght)
A drift of bees; of birds; of cattle; of dust; of fishers; of fishing nets; of ice; of sand; of sheep; of smoke; of snow; drift of anglers; of swans.

DRIVE (collection of objects or animals driven, *syn* drift, drove)
Drive of cattle; of logs.

DROVE (number of cattle or other animals driven in a body, a crowd of people moving in one direction, *syn* drift, flock, concourse)
Drove of asses; of hares; of bullocks; of cattle; of heresies; of immoralities; of kine; of oxen; of sheep; of swine.

DRUGGERY (drugs, *collectively*)

DRUM (a noisy assembly of society in a private house)

DRUNKENSHIP of cobblers (cobblers, *collectively*)

DRYFT of tame swine (a herd)

DUET of doves, turkeys (two or more birds)

DULE of doves (alternative of dole of doves)

EARTH (all people on the globe, *collectively*, *also* a group of foxes)

ECHELLE (in ladder form)
An echelle of ribbons.

ECHELON (an arrangement of troops drawn up in parallel lines in step formation, vessels advancing in line at an angle to the direction)

EDITION (the number of copies of a book or paper printed at the one time)

EIGHT (a rowing crew)

ELEVEN (a cricket or football team, *collectively*)

ELOQUENCE of lawyers (15th century, lawyers, *collectively*)

EMBRACING of carvers (15th century)

EMBROIDERY (a diversity or exaggeration)
An embroidery of courtesy; of humour; of lies; of poetic dreams; of wild flowers.

ENTRANCE of actresses (modern)

EPISCOPATE (the body of bishops)

ERST of bees

ERUDITION of editors (modern pun)

ESCARGATOIRE (a nursery of snails)

ESCORT (a body of armed men who accompany someone or something of importance, also who appear in public ceremonies to escort the Queen in procession)

ESCHEAT of lawyers (modern pun)

ESTABLISHMENT (the civil, military or political body or organisation in a county, *also* an establishment, a household)

EXAGGERATION of fishermen (modern pun)

EXALTATION of larks (a flock)

EXAMPLE of masters (15th century)

EXECUTION of officers (15th century)

EXUBERANCE (superabundance, overflowing quantity; outburst, *syn* abundance, plenteousness)
An exuberance of spirits; of fancy; of foliage; of joy.

EYE (a brood, as of pheasants, *also* nye)

EYRAR (a brood of swans)

EYRIE *See* AERIE.

FACTION (a company of people acting together, usually a contentious party, a set or class of people, *syn* clique, cabal, junto)

FACTORY (a body of factors or workers, now obsolete)

FACULTY (a body of persons entrusted with the government and tuition in a college or university, *also* members of a particular profession regarded as a body)
Faculty of advocates.

FADGE (a bundle or bale of leather, sticks, wool, etc.)

FAGGOT (bundle or bunch of anything, also a bundle of material used for fuel, *syn* fascine)
A faggot of compliments; of herbs; of rushes; of selections; of sticks; of twigs; utter improbabilities.

FAITH of merchants (15th century, company of merchants)

FALL (quantity born or produced at one time or within a certain period, *syn* brood, cast, clutch)
A fall of hail; of lambs; of meteors; of rain; of snow; of spawn; of woodcock.

FAMILY (a group or assembly of objects connected by some common feature or property; a troop or school, a body of servants of a house, the members of a family, *syn* clan, set)
A family of curves; of gladiators; of legends; of myths; of thieves.

FANGOT (a quantity of goods, in particular silk)

FARE (a company ready to travel, a troop, a multitude or swarm, a catch of fish)
A fare of flatterers, fools and cheaters; of flies (a swarm); of pigs (a litter)

FARDEL (a bundle or pack)
A fardel of sin; of sorrow.

FARRAGO (a confused mixture, a medley, *syn* hotchpotch)
A farrago of cowardice; of cunning; of doubts; of fears; of hopes; of lies; of wishes.

FASCICLE (a small bundle or collection, a compact cluster)
Fascicle of fibres; of flowers; of leaves (making up a section of a book being published section by section); of roots; of virtue.

FASCICULE (a handful)

FASCINE (a long cylindrical bundle, as of sticks of wood bound together; used in dams, jetties, etc.)

FATHOM (a quantity of wood (six foot square in section))

FAWNING of courtiers (15th century, a group of courtiers)

FEAST (collectively the company at a feast)
A feast of brewers; of guests.

FEC (a quantity, especially the greater part, *syn* bulk)

FEDERATION (a league, confederacy)

FELLOWRED (a company of fellows)

FELLOWSHIP (a company of equals or friends, a union or association, *syn* fraternity, brotherhood)
Fellowship of apostles; of vessels; of yeomen.

FERKIN (a measure of quantity, half a kilderkin (1465))

FERMENT (a tumult of agitation, a group or crowd of people so affected)

FERNERY (collection of ferns)

FESNYNG of ferrets (a pack of ferrets, 15th century, *also* fesynes)

FESTOON (a chain or garland of things suspended)
A festoon of banners; of cobwebs; of flowers; of ivy; of ribbon.

FESTOONERY (a group of objects arranged in festoons)

FIELD (the collective name of all competitors in a sporting contest or horse race; a stretch or expanse)
Field of clouds; of cricketers; of hunting horses; of miracles; of raillery; of runners; of stars; of woes.

FIFTEEN (a rugby team)

FIGHTING of beggars (15th century)

FILE (an orderly collection of papers arranged in sequence, a row of persons, animals or things arranged one behind the other, a small number of soldiers)
A file of letters; of newspapers; of papers; of soldiers (two deep)

FINERY (a collection of things finely made, rich wearing apparel)

FIRLOT (a measure of corn, the fourth part of a boll, *also* a great quantity)

FISHERY (a group of fishermen)

FLAKE (a bundle of parallel fibres or threads)

FLAP of nuns (modern pun)

FLAW (turfs, *collectively*)

FLEET (a number of ships or vessels in company; *collectively*, the naval force of a country, *also* group of lorries, etc.)

A fleet of aircraft; of birds; of motorcars; of ships; of mudhens; of lorries.

FLICK (collective term for rabbits or hares)

FLIGHT (a number of things or beings passing through the air together, a series of objects resembling a flight of stairs or series, as of canal locks, a flock flying in company, *syn* skein, bevy, covey)
A flight of academicians; of aeroplanes; of airmen; of angels; of birds (young birds which have taken flight together); of clouds; of doves; of dunbirds; of fish-hooks (used in spinning trace); of goshawks; of hurdles (athletics); of locks (canals); of pigeons; of rails; of steps; of storks; of swallows; of terraces; of cormorants; of dunlin; of larks; of plover; of widgeon; of woodcock.

FLING (a flock of dunlin or other sandpipers)
A fling of dunbirds; of oxbirds.

FLOCK (a company of people, birds or animals, domestic animals, *also* all Christians, *syn* bevy, drove)
A flock of affections; of auks (at sea); of birds; of bitterns; of Christians; of coots; of cranes; of parrots; of camels; of fish; of lice; of bustards; of elephants; of friends; of geese; of goats; of lions; of pamphlets; of prophets; of seals; of sheep; of swifts;

FLOE (a field or pack of ice)

FLOOD (a great flow or stream of any fluid, any great overwhelming quantity)
A flood of bank notes; of fiery words; of lava; of light; of tears; of visitors, *also* floods of eloquence.

FLORILEGIUM (a collection of flowers; of poetic passages, *syn* anthology)

FLOTE (a fleet or flotilla, a company or troop, a herd of cattle or a shoal of fish)

FLOTILLA (a small fleet or a fleet of small vessels, *syn* flote, armada)
A flotilla of boats; of destroyers; of proverbs.

FLOURISH of strumpets.

FLOWERAGE (flowers, *collectively*)

FLURRY (a fluttering assembly of things)
A flurry of birds (fluttering around before setting out, or when settling down on a lake or marsh); of rain; of snowflakes; of wind.

FLUSH (a flock of startled birds; a hand of cards of the same suit, a sudden abundant growth of emotion)
A flush of wing commanders; of plumbers (modern pun); of mallard.

FLUTHER of jellyfish

FLUTTER of cardiologists (modern pun)

FOLD (a flock which is enclosed within a fence or shelter, a congregation or group of Christians)
A fold of sheep.

FOLK (people in general, or a special class, persons of one's own family, kinfolk)

FOLKMOOT *or* **FOLKMOTE** (a general meeting of people belonging to a town or city)

FOLLOWING (followers, adherents, *collectively*)

FOND (a stock of money or of goods, *syn* store)

FONT *see* **FOUNT**

FOOLIAMINY (a body of fools)

FORCE (a body of men prepared for action, *syn* army, host, troop)

FORESIGHT of housekeepers (15th century)

FOREST (an extensive wood, also used figuratively)
Forest of posts; of spires; of scaffolding; of telegraph poles; of trees; of verbal arguments.

FORMATION (a formal assembly of troops, an arrangement of rocks in a geological sense)

FOUNT *or* **FONT** (assortment of type of one size and style)

FOUNTAIN (a jet or stream of liquid, also used figuratively, *syn* spring)

FOUR (polo team, rowing crew)

FRAIL (a quantity of raisins)

FRAME of waggons (a number travelling together)

FRAPE (a crowd, an unruly mob)

FRATERNITY (a group of men associated by a common interest, *syn* brotherhood, fellowship, guild)

FRATRY (a fraternity, *also* a convent of friars)

FRAUNCH of milliners (15th century, fraunch means to eat ravenously)

FRIARY (a brotherhood of friars)

FRITH (woods or wooded country, *collectively*)

FROGGERY (a gathering of frogs)

FRONDAGE (fronds, *collectively*, leafy foliage)

FROST of dowagers (modern pun)

FRUITAGE *or* **FRUITERY** (fruit, *collectively*)

FRUSH (fragments, splinters, *collectively*)

FRY (the young or hatched brood of fishes, *also* the young or brood of other animals or insects such as oysters or bees, *syn* swarm or brood)
Fry of authors; of bees (young); of eels (spawns); of foul decays; of islands; of oysters (young).

FULLAGE (collected refuse, street sweepings)

FURORE of bandsmen.

FUSILLADE (a simultaneous discharge of firearms; also used figuratively)
Fusillade of bullets; of personalities; of terror; of swearing.

FUSION (a union or blending of things, *syn* coalition)

GAGGLE (a flock of geese, a company of women, *syn* giggle)

GALAXY (an assembly of brilliant or noted persons or things, *syn* constellation)
Galaxy of astronomers; of governesses; of stars.

GALE (a state of current of passing emotions, perfume or similar intangible things)
A gale of doubts and apprehension; of fragrance; of laughter; of merriment; of opportunity; of perfumes; of praise.

GALERE (a group of persons, a clique)

GALLERY (the audience in the gallery, used in relation to the musical hall or the political arena, i.e. 'playing to the gallery', *syn* audience)

GALLIMAUFRY (a medley, a hotchpotch of things or people)

GAM (a herd or school of whales, also whaling ships in company)
Gam of porpoises.

GAME (a flock or herd of animals raised and kept for sport or pleasure)
A game of bees; of conies; of red deer; players in a game; of swans.

GANG (a full set of things or persons, a group of persons doing the same work, *syn* company, set)
A gang of cartwheels (set of four); of chronographers;

of clerks; of convicts; of coopers; of dogs; of elks; of heretics; of horse-shoes; of oars; of ploughs; of ruffians; of saws; of shrouds (set of sails); of slaves; of thieves; of workmen.

GARB (a bundle, *syn* gavel, glean, sheaf)
A garb of oats; of steel rods; of wheat.

GARLAND (a collection of extracts, songs, etc., *syn* chaplet)
A garland of ballads; of flowers; of songs.

GARLANDRY (a collection of garlands)

GARNISH (a set of dishes, etc., for the table)

GARRISON (a body of soldiers stationed at a town or place for its defence)

GATE (a number of people admitted to a sporting event)

GATHERING (a crowd, assembly, collection)

GAVEL (a quantity of mown grain to make a sheaf; a bundle of hay, rushes or similar grasses, *syn* math)

GEAR (property in general, person's things, such as clothes, *collectively*)

GENERALITY (the generals in an army, *collectively*)

GENERATION (a race, family, offspring or descendants)

GENTRY (person of upper class, *collectively*)

GENUS (a class, order or type of things)

GERONTOCRACY (a government by old men)

GIGGLE (pun on gaggle)
Giggle of girls; giggle of typists.

GING (a gang, a troop, a crew, *also* a retinue of servants or the people in a household)

GIRDLE (something that encircles or confines, *syn* circle, chain)
Girdle of din (noises); of forest; of perfection; of snow.

GIRLERY *or* **GIRLHOOD** (girls, *collectively*)

GLARING of cats.

GLEAN (a sheaf or bundle of a commodity which has been gleaned, *syn* garb)
A glean of grain; of hemp; of herrings.

GLOAT of examiners (modern pun)

GLOBE (a body of people or soldiers drawn up in a circle, *syn* ball, clew, orb)

GNOMOLOGY (a collection of maxims and moral sentences)

GOOD ADVICE of burgesses (15th century)

GOOSERY (geese, *collectively*)

GORING of butchers (15th century, butchers, *collectively*)

GOSSIPING (gossips, *collectively*)

GOWN (collectively the students of a university as opposed to the citizens of the town who are known as the 'town', *also* lawyers, *collectively*)

GRAFT of tree surgeons (modern pun)

GREAT BEVY of roe deer (twelve head of deer)

GRECE (steps or stairs, *collectively*)

GRIND (a school of blackfish, *also* of bottlenosed whales)

GRIST (a lot, a quantity, a supply for an occasion)
A grist of bees; of grain (as much as is carried to the mill at one time); of meal; of flies.

GROUP (a set of things collected as a unit, *syn* gathering)
A group of columns (three or four columns joined together on the same pedestal); of islands; of musicians; of singers; of trees; of woes; of words.

GROVE (a small grove of trees or something similar, *syn* bosquet)
A grove of bayonets; of spears; of trees.

GUARD (a body of men positioned to protect or control, *syn* escort)

GUESS of diagnosticians (modern pun)

GUILD (an association of men or women belonging to the same class or engaged in the same industry or profession, *syn* fraternity, association, union)

GULP of swallows.

GUNNERY (guns, *collectively*)

GUSH (a sudden outflowing, *syn* outburst, abundance)
A gush of water.

GUST (a sudden outburst, *syn* rack)

GUZZLE of aldermen.

HAGGLE of vendors (shopkeepers, *collectively*)

HAIL (a storm or shower of anything similar to hail, *syn* fusillade)
Hail of bullets; of shots.

HAND (a round of applause, something resembling a hand in appearance or function, *syn* bunch)
Hand of applause; of bananas; of bridge.

HARAS (a stud, a breed of horses)
Haras of breeding mares; of wild horses.

HAREM (a family of wives, concubines, female relatives and servants)

HARL (a leash of hounds, three in number, *also* a small quantity)

HARVEST (season's yield of any natural product, *also* figuratively)
Harvest of grouse; of hate; of mice; of peace.

HASTINESS of cooks (cooks, *collectively*)

HAUL (a single draft of fish, that which is caught or taken at one time, *syn* catch, cast)

HEAD (a collection of animals, an indefinite number, a bundle of flax or silk)
A head of hungry wolves; of pheasants; of cattle (used numerically, e.g. a thousand head of cattle)

HEAP (a pile or mass, collection of things thrown together, a crowd, a large number)
A heap of castles; of ideas; of islands; of learned men; of servants; of sins; of trouble.

HEATHENRY (the heathen of the world, *collectively*)

HEAVEN (the assembly of the blessed, *collectively*)

HEAVENWARE (inmates of heaven)

HELOTRY (slaves or bondsmen, *collectively*)

HERBARIUM (a collection of dried plants or herbs)

HERBARY (a garden of herbs or vegetables, *also* a collection of herbs)

HERD (a number of animals assembled together, chiefly large animals, *also* a crowd of common people, *syn* flock, rabble)
A herd of antelopes; of asses; of attributes; of bison; of boars; of buffalo; of camels; of caribou; of cattle; of chamois; of cranes; of curlew; of deer; of elephants; of giraffes; of goats; of harlots; of harts; of ibex; of moose; of oxen; of parasites; of ponies; of porpoises; of seals; of swans; of swine; of sycophants; of whales; of wrens.

HERITAGE (heirs, *collectively*)

HIERARCHY (a body of officials arranged in ranks, each rank subordinate to the one above)

HILL (a heap of earth raised about the roots of crops, therefore the crops themselves)
A hill of corn; of potatoes; of ruffs.

HIVE of bees or oysters.

HOARD (a stock or store accumulated)
A hoard of coins; of facts; of grace; of grievance; of provisions; of secrets.

HODGEPODGE, *see* HOTCHPOTCH.

HOGGERY (hogs, *collectively*)

HOI POLLOI (the masses, the common people, *syn* commonalty)

HORDE (a great company, especially of savage or uncivilized people, *syn* a gang, troop)
A horde of barbarians; of insects; of misers; of pirates; of regicides; of savages; of urchins; of wolves; of young readers; of gnats.

HOST (an army; a large number of men; a great multitude, *syn* force, troop)
A host of angels; of arguments; of books; of daffodils; of debaters; of facts; of hoteliers (pun on the name for an innkeeper); of images; of men; of monks; of odds and ends; of questions; of sparrows; of thoughts; of trunks.

HOSTING (a muster of armed men)

HOTCHPOTCH (a confused mixture)
A hotchpotch of errors; of ideas; of tastes.

HOUSE (an assembly of legislative or deliberative persons, *syn* assembly)
House of Commons; of Lords; of Representatives.

HOVER of trout (waiting for food); of crows.

HUDDLE (a number of persons or things crowded together, *syn* jumble, conglomeration)
Huddle of puppies; of chances; of ideas; of large stones; of walruses.

HUMANITY (human beings, *collectively*)

HURRY (a small load of hay or corn)

HURTLE (a flock of sheep)

HUSKE (a down or group of hares)

HUTTING (huts, *collectively*)

ILLUSION of painters (15th century)

IMBROGLIO (a confused heap of things)

INCREDIBILITY of cuckolds (15th century)

INDIFFERENCE of waiters (modern)

INGRATITUDE of children (modern)

INSTITUTE (an organization for the promotion of learning, *syn* institution, society)

INSTITUTION (an established or organized society or corporation, *syn* foundation)

JAM of tarts (modern pun on a group of prostitutes)

JEWRY (Jews, *collectively*)

JOBBERY (jobs or work, *collectively*)

JOINT of osteopaths (modern pun)

JORUM (a large quantity, a large drinking vessel and its contents)

JOURNEY of coins (a batch minted together, also 720 ounces or 2,000 gold coins)

JUDICATURE *or* **JUDICIARY** (the judges of a country, *collectively*)

JUG (to nestle or collect in a covey, therefore the covey itself)
A jug of grouse (roosting); of partridge; of quail.

JUMBLE (a confused mixture, *syn* huddle, hotchpotch)
A jumble of words.

JUNTA *or* **JUNTO** (a group of men united together for some secret intrigue, *syn* cabal, conspiracy)
Junto of gods; of ministers; of wise men; of wits.

JURY (a company of persons whose duty is to reach a verdict in a trial, or to judge and award prizes in a competitive event, *also* a dozen men)

KELP (a collective name for seaweeds which are to be burnt or processed)

KENDLE, *see* KINDLE.

KENNEL (a pack of hounds, dogs or other animals, *also* applied to persons, *syn* crew, gang)

KILDERKIN (a measured capacity, usually the fourth part of a tun)

KINDRED (relatives *collectively*)

KINDLE (*also* kendle, kindling or kyndyll; a litter or brood) A kindle of hares; of kittens; of leverets; of rabbits.

KIP (a set or bundle of hides or young or small beasts, i.e. calves or lambs)

KIPPAGE (a ship's crew or company)

KITCHENRY (the group of servants engaged in the kitchen, *collectively*)

KNIGHTAGE *or* **KNIGHTHOOD** (knights, *collectively*)

KNITCH (a bundle of wood, hay, corn, etc., tied together, *syn* a sheaf or faggot)

KNITCHET (a small handful, such as of reeds)

KNOB of pochard; of widgeon (on water)

KNOT (a small cluster or group of persons or things) A knot of clubs (social); of idioms; of islands; of mountains (where mountain chains meet); of palm trees; of people;

of politicians; of roots (personal links and environment); of separatists; of small stars; of talk; of thread or yarn; of toads; of witches; of young snakes; of astrologers.

KYNDYLL, *see* KINDLE.

LABOUR of moles (15th century)

LAC (a great number, *also* more specifically 100,000)
A lac of islands; of pagodas; of rupees.

LADYHOOD (ladies, *collectively*)

LAITY (laymen, *collectively*, *also* non-professionals as opposed to professionals)

LANDLORDRY (landlords, *collectively*)

LAP (a bundle, also the amount a thing overlaps)

LASH of carters (15th century)

LAST (a load or burden, an amount of cod or herring (12 barrels), *also* a measure of grain or malt (80 bushels), a large indefinite number)

LATROCINY (a band of robbers 1738)

LAUGHTER (a clutch of eggs)
A laughter of eggs; of ostlers (15th century)

LAYER (a substance or things grouped together and lying between two other horizontal strata)

LAYETTE (an outfit and toilet materials for a baby or young child)

LEA (a measure of yarn which varies according to type, i.e., worsted (80 yards); cotton (120 yards))

LEAFAGE (leaves, *collectively*, *syn* foliage)

LEAGUE (a group of persons, states or other organizations with a common interest)
A league of princes; the League of Nations.

LEAP of banderilleros (modern); of leopards.

LEASE (three, alternative of leash)
Lease of hares; of thread; of fish.

LEASH (a sporting term, a brace and a half, a tierce, i.e., three)
A leash of bucks; of days; of deer; of foxes; of greyhounds; of hares; of hawks; of kings; of partridges; of snipe; of teal; of trout; of hounds.

LECE of greyhound (three, *syn* leash)
A lece of hawks.

LEDE (persons, *collectively*, one's own people, race or nation)

LEER of boys (modern)

LEGATION (a group of diplomats sent on a mission or stationed in a foreign country, *also* Legacy, a body of delegates or papal legates)

LEGENDRY (legends, *collectively*)

LEGION (a multitude, a great number, a Roman unit of troops, a host of armed men)
A legion of angels; of devils; of passions; of reproaches; of whelps.

LEGISLATURE (a body of persons elected or invested with the power to make laws)

LEK (a gathering, as in sport)
A lek of black grouse.

LEPE (a group of leopards)

LEVEE (a reception often held in the morning, therefore any miscellaneous gathering of guests)

LEVESEL (a bower of leaves, a canopy or lattice)

LEVY (a collection together of things levied; a meeting of scholars on some matter relating to the school)
Levy of money; of troops

LIBRARY (a collection of books, therefore a collection of knowledge)
A library of law; of opinions; of reasons.

LINE (a series or rank of objects or persons, usually of the same kind)
A line of barriers; of geese (a flock); of trading posts; of type (printing).

LINGERIE (linen articles, *collectively*, now chiefly the underclothes of a woman)

LIST (a number of names, words or figures written together)

LITTER (the young brought forth at one time by a sow or similar animal, a disorderly cumulation of papers)
Litter of kittens; of puppies.

LITTLE HERD (20 head of deer)

LIVERY (retainers, *collectively*)

LOAD (a great amount, a quantity, *syn* burden, charge)
Load of drunks; of guilt; of trouble; of woes.

LOBBY (collectively those who visit Members of Parliament to influence the way they will vote or speak)

LOCK (a handful, armful or small bundle)
A lock of bacon; of clover; of flax; of hair; of ham; of money; of straw.

LOCKET (a group of set jewels)

LODGE (a collection of objects lodged or close together, a family unit of four or six persons, *also* the body of members of a masonic or other society)
Lodge of beavers; of islands; of masons; of otters.

LOFT (a flock of pigeons)

LOT (a number of persons or things taken collectively, *syn* back, sort, break)
A lot of bother; of cattle; of stationery.

LUMP (a great quantity, the majority)

LURCH of buses (modern)

LURRY (a confused group, or sound of voices, *syn* hubbub)
A lurry of people; of opinions.

LUTE (a flock of mallard)

LYING of pardoners (15th century)

MACARONI (a medley, poetic selections)

MADDER of painters (modern pun)

MALPERTNESS of pedlars (15th century)

MANHOOD (men, *collectively*)

MANTLE (a quantity of furs)

MANY (a large number)

MASS (a large quantity, the whole quantity or the larger amount, *syn* bulk, majority)
Mass of bruises; of colours; of evidence; of faults; of folly; of heresies; of mistakes; of priests; of sand; of treasures; of water.

MATH (an amount of mown grass)

MEDLEY (a mixture, jumble, hodgepodge, a mixed literary collection, a composition of parts of different pieces of music)
Medley of sounds; of tunes; of voices.

MEET (the persons or group of horsemen and women who gather for a foxhunt or other sporting events)
A meet of cyclists; of huntsmen.

MEETING (a public gathering; a race meeting, etc.)

MEINY *or* **MEINIE** (family, body of attendants, company of people employed together, a great number, *syn* train, retinue, flock)
Meiny of brooks; of chessmen (a set); of oxen; of pilgrims; of plants; of sheep; of sparrows; of villains.

MELLAY (a mixture, usually of coloured items)

MELLEFICIUM (a collection of quotations, *syn* macaroni, miscellany)

MELODY of harpers (15th century)

MENAGE (members of a household, members of a club or benefit society)

MENAGERIE (a collection of wild or foreign animals, *also* an aviary)

MERCHANTRY (merchants, *collectively*)

MESS (a confused mixture; a group of four; a group of people who regularly eat together; the quantity of milk at one milking, a quantity of food)
Mess of beans; of judges or barristers (when on circuit); of mackerel; of marines; of milk; of officers; of peas; of potage; of sons (four); of strawberries; of victuals; of vinegar.

MEUTE (pack of hounds, *alternative* of meuse or mews)

MEWS (stable for horses, a collection of hawks moulting or hens and capons fattening)

MICKLE (a small amount used in the phrase 'many a mickle makes a muckle', apparently the use of muckle is not accepted by the O.E.D. who quotes 'many a pickle makes a mickle')

MIDDEN (an accumulation of refuse)

MIDDLE BEVY (ten head of roe deer, or forty head of deer in general)

MIGRATION (collectively the persons, mammals or birds which take part in a migratory movement abroad)

MINSTRELSY (collective body of minstrels of musicians, musical instruments, *collectively*, *syn* consort)
The minstrelsy of heaven.

MINISTRY (Christian ministers or clergy, *collectively*; the group of ministers of state)

MINT (a vast sum of money, or of something equally costly)
A mint of bravery; of money; of phrases; of reasons.

MISBELIEF of painters (15th century)

MISCELLANEA (collection of miscellaneous matter, e.g., a literary miscellanea)

MISCELLANY (mixture of various things, a medley, collection of writings on various subjects)
Miscellany of deformities; of humours; of prose.

MOB (a rabble, a crowd or collection of things, *syn* flock, herd or canaille)
Mob of books; of ducks; of horses; of kangaroos; of metaphors; of people; of sheep; of thoughts; of whales.

MOIETY (a half, the better half or a small part)

MONKDOM *or* **MONKERY, MONKSHIP** (monks, *collectively*)

MONTAGE (a musical composite of heterogeneous sounds or fragment of music, *also* a quick succession of bursts of dialogue, or music and sound effect used to link a gap in time in a play, opera, etc.)

MONTE *or* **MONTY** (the pile of cards left after each player has taken his share)

MOP (something likened to a mop) a mop of hair

MORRIS (a group of morris dancers)

MORT (East Anglian *dialect* for a lot)

MOTORCADE (a procession of motor vehicles)

MOW (a heap of hay)

MUCKLE, *see* MICKLE.

MUDDLE (a confused collection, *syn* jumble)

MULADA (a drove of mules)

MULTIPLYING of husbands.

MULTITUDE (a great number, a host of persons or things, *syn* army)
Multitude of cares; of favours; of people; of questions; of sins; of stars.

MURDER of crows (a flock)

MURMURATION of starlings (a flock)

MUSKETRY (muskets, *collectively*)

MUSTER (a number of persons or things assembled on a particular occasion, *syn* levy)
Muster of peacocks; of troops; mustering of storks.

MUTATION of thrushes (group of moulting birds)

MUTE (pack of hounds)

MYRIAD (a countless number of persons, or animals or things, specifically a group of 10,000 items)

NABOBERY (Nabobs of India, *collectively*)

NATION (the inhabitants of a country, a community of men or animals, *syn* a multitude, host)

NAVY (a fleet of ships, sailors, *collectively*)

NEST (a number or collection of people, a number of birds or insects occupying the same place, an accumulation of similar objects, a number of buildings or streets, a set of objects, *syn* aeries, brood, bike)

A nest of alleys (closely built alleyways); of arguments; of boxes (which fit one inside the other); of caterpillars; of chicken; of crocodiles; of dormice; of evils; of fools; of goblets; of hedgehogs; of hummocks; of kittens; of low bushes; of mice; of miracles; of night-caps; of outlaws; of pirates; of profaneness; of quiet streets; of rabbits; of robbers; of rumours; of shelves; of tables; of toads; of traitors; of trotters; of wasps; of wharfs; of vipers.

NETWORK (collection or arrangement of items to resemble a net, *syn* framework)
Network of canals; of islands; of lines; of pearls; of railways; of rivers; of ropes; of trenches; of veins; of wrinkles.

NEVER-THRIVING of jugglers (15th century)

NIDE (a nest or brood of young birds, *syn* bike)
Nide of eggs; of geese; of pheasants.

NIEVEFUL (a handful)
Nieveful of prunes.

NINE (a baseball team)

NON-PATIENCE of wives (15th century)

NOSEGAY (bunch of fragrant flowers or herbs, *syn* bouquet)

NUCLEUS (a central mass or number, a collection of persons or items to which addition will be made)
Nucleus of physicists (modern pun)

NUNNERY (a company of nuns)

NYE, *see* NIDE.

OBEISANCE of servants (15th century)

OBSCURATION of dons (academics, *collectively*)

OBSERVANCE (a religious order such as the Franciscans who observe or follow a rule, *syn* confession, rule)
An observance of hermits.

OBSTINACY of buffaloes.

ODIUM of politicians (modern)

OLIO (a collection of miscellaneous pieces, a hotchpotch, a medley, a pot-pourri)
Olio of affairs; of musical pieces; of pictures; of various religions; of verses.

OMLAH (a body or group of native officials)

OMNIBUS (a group of large number and great variety of objects, persons or societies)

OMNIUM GATHERUM (quasi-Latin for a gathering, a medley or collection of several types)

ONCOME (a heavy fall, *syn* outburst)
Oncome of rain; of snow.

ONOMASTICON (vocabulary or collection of names)

OODLE *or* **OODLIN** (a mass of things, a heap, a great quantity, usually in the plural)
Oodles of food; of money; of time.

OPTIENCE (a group of spectators as at a cinema show)

OPUS (a musical composition *or* collection of compositions)

ORB (a collective whole, a circle of things or people, *syn* ball, globe)
Orb of soldiers; of witnesses.

ORCHESTRA (a group of performers on various instruments, distinguished from a band and from groups such as the quartet, septet, etc., *also* used to describe a collective sound which is reminiscent of an orchestra playing, such as the sound of the sea, or the wind)

ORDER (a body or society of persons united by a common rule, a monastic society, any of the nine grades of angels, *syn* rank, row, series)

OSTENTATION of peacocks.

OUTBURST (*syn* outgush)
Outburst of weeping.

OUTFIT (the articles forming an equipment or clothing, e.g., a bridal outfit, or policemen's outfit, persons forming a party engaged in herding, mining, etc., *also* any group of persons in a particular industry or pursuit)
Outfit of clothes; of sails.

OUTGUSH (*syn* outburst)
Outgush of emotion.

PACE of asses (a herd)

PACK (a bundle of things enclosed or tied together, a company or set of persons, a large collection or set of things, a number of animals, *syn* bundle or bolt)
Pack of books; of cards; of coal (3 Winchester bushels); of complaints; of dogs; of fools; of grouse; of heresies; of hounds; of ice; of icebergs; of Jews; of knaves; of lies; of nonsense; of perch; of schoolboys; of sorrows; of stoats; of superstitions; of weasels; of witches; of wolves.

PACKAGE (a bundle of things packed together)

PAD (a bunch or package, a mass of anything soft, i.e., a cushion)
A pad of writing paper; of wool; of yarn; *also* a pad of mackerel (a measure of sixty mackerel)

PADDLING of ducks.

PALISADE (anything resembling or likened to a row of stakes)
Palisade of cliffs; of ice pinnacles; of mountains; of shrubs; of stakes; of stiff hairs; of trees.

PALLOR of nightwatchmen (modern)

PANDEMONIUM (a place or gathering of wild persons, originally denoted hell)
Pandemonium of devils; of iniquity.

PANEL (a list of people, also the people themselves)
Panel of experts; of judges; of jurymen; of patients.

PANTHEON of Gods (Gods, *collectively*)

PARADE (a procession of animals or people, *syn* cortège, procession)
Parade of firemen; of elephants; of soldiers.

PARCEL (a small amount, a small party, company or collection of persons or animals or things, articles for sale, *syn* bundle)
Parcel of bachelors; of blockheads; of brutes; of crows; of diamonds; of fair dames; of girls; of hens and chickens; of horses; of ideas; of land; of mathematicians; of lies; of linnets; of money; of observations; of penguins; of people; of sheep; of woes; of wry faces.

PARE (parings, *collectively*, the amount pared or cut off)
A pare of men.

PAREL (an army)
Parel of troops.

PARENTAGE (parents, *collectively*)

PARK (a space occupied by parked vehicles, stores, etc., hence the objects themselves, *collectively*)
Artillery park; carpark; park of waggons.

PARLIAMENT of owls; of fowls.

PARTY (company or body of persons; detachment of troops; a group of people travelling together, a gathering for social entertainment, *syn* set, clique)
Party of birds; of jays; of pleasures; of politicians.

PASH (a heavy fall of rain or snow, a great number of fragments, *syn* fall, oncome)

PASSAGE (herons in flight are 'on passage')

PASSEL (alternative for parcel, e.g., the American passel of brats)

PASTICHE *or* **PASTICCIO** (a medley, potpourri or hodgepodge)

PAT (a small mass of soft substance, formed or shaped by patting)
A pat of butter; of water.

PATCH (a collection or mass of floating ice flows)

PATROL (detachment of troops or police, *syn* guard)

PAVANNE of matadors (modern pun)

PEAL (succession of loud sounds)
Peal of artillery; of bells; of laughter; of thunder.

PEASANTRY (peasants, *collectively*)

PECK (a measured quantity of both dry or wet substance, *also* more generally a considerable quantity or number)
A peck of bees; of pepper; of troubles.

PEEP (a brood of chicken)

PEERAGE (the body of peers)

PELTRY (pelts or skins, *collectively*, *also* refuse, rubbish, trash)

PENCIL (a small tuft, a slender cylinder of articles formed into the shape of a pencil)
Pencil of feathers; of hairs; of light rays.

PENTAD (a group of five, *especially* of five years)

PEOPLE (human beings, *collectively*)

PERSISTANCE of parents.

PEWAGE *or* **PEWING** (church pews, *collectively*)

PHALANSTERY (a group or association of people or persons, *esp* those following the plan of Fourierism)
Phalanstery of all the fiends.

PHALANX (compact group of people or animals prepared for attack or for defence, *also* any body of persons or things drawn together in a common purpose)
Phalanx of elms; infantry; lawyers; of migrating storks.

PHANTASMAGORIE (a series of phantoms or imagined figures)
A phantasmagorie of bright colours; of contending angels; of feathers; of spangles; of figures; of ghosts or phantoms.

PHANTOMTRY (phantoms or ghosts, *collectively*)

PHRASEOLOGY (collection or handbook of phrases)

PICKET (a detached body of men, *syn* detachment, detail)
Picket of soldiers; of strikers.

PICKLE (a small amount, *see* MICKLE)

PIE (a collection of things made into a heap; a confused mass, *syn* jumble, *also* a collection of rules)
Pie of coals; of manure; of potatoes; of type (when the printing forme has been broken down)

PIECE (a portion or quantity, a length)
Piece of calico (ten yards); of muslin (twelve yards)

PILE (a heap of things of some height, a large group, clump or collection of things, *syn* bank, balk)
Pile of arms or weapons; of islands; of money; of shot; of stones; of trees; of wood.

PILLAR (upright pillar-like mass, *syn* column)
Pillar of air; of cloud; of sand; of type (printing); of smoke; of vapour; of water.

PILLARING (pillars, *collectively*)

PINCH (a very small quantity)
Pinch of pleasure; of salt; of snuff.

PIPAGE (pipes, *collectively*)

PITTANCE (a small portion, number or amount)
A pittance of food; of grace; of learning; of money; of reasoning.

PITY of prisoners (a group of prisoners)

PLAGUE (a group which, by their size and nature, cause devastation or irritation)
Plague of gnats; of infidels; of locusts.

PLATE (tableware, *collectively*)

PLATOON (a squad, a company or set of persons)
Platoon of arguments; of gunfire (a number of shots fired simultaneously); of troops.

PLEBS (the common people, *from* the Roman use of plebeian)

PLEIAD (a brilliant cluster or group, of persons or things)
Pleiad of poets; of writers; of stars.

PLUCK (a cluster or group of things plucked)
A pluck of shawmers (i.e., a group of players of the shawm, a medieval musical instrument)

PLUMP (a compact body of persons, animals or things, *syn* a troop, flock)
A plump of conjectures and presumptions; of ducks; of men; of moorhens; of pains; of seals; of spears (also spearmen, *collectively*); of trees (a clump); of yachts; of whales; of wild fowl.

POCKET (a collection or small quantity, as of ore, *syn* layer)
Pocket of air; of hops (168 lb.); of nuggets (of gold); of earth; of water.

POD (small herd or school of birds or mammals)
Pod of birds; of coots; of seals; of whales; of whiting; of porpoises.

POESY (a bunch or nosegay, *syn* posy)
A poesy of flowers.

POMP (a procession or pageant)
A pomp of pekinese (modern)

PONTIFICALITE (prelates, *collectively*)

POOL (small body of liquids; a reservoir or persons or things)
A pool of blood; of sunlight; of typists; of water.

POPULACE (the majority, the common people, *syn* mob)

PORT (a train or retinue of attendants)

PORTFOLIO of brokers (modern pun)

POSE (a hoard, a secret store)
Pose of treasure.

POSSE (a company or force with legal authority, a strong band of persons, animals, etc.)
A posse of articles (literary); of cock turkeys; of constables; of enthusiasts; of hell; of police; of ranters; of sheriffs; of silly women.

POSSE COMITATUS (the body of men over the age of fifteen which the sheriff of an English county could raise in a crisis)

POSTIL (collection of homilies)

POSY (a collection or bouquet of flowers, of poetry or rhetoric, *syn* posey)
Posy of comic stories.

POT (a mass of material filling a pot-hole, a large sum of money, a conventional quantity or measure)
A pot of apples (five pecks); of butter (fourteen lb.); of money; of sugar (70 lb.).

POTPOURRI (a medley or collection of musical or literary extracts)
Potpourri of sounds; of flower perfumes.

POUNDING of pianists (modern)

POVERTY (poor people, *collectively*)
Poverty of pipers; of paupers.

POWER (a large number, an abundance, a body of armed men, a fighting force)
Power of angels; of followers; of goods; of good things; of money; of years.

PRANCE of equestrians (modern pun on horse-riders)

PRELACY (prelates, *collectively*)

PRESBYTERY (a body of elders of the church)

PRESS (a crush of people, the newspaper reporters, *collectively*, as much sail as the wind will permit a ship to carry, a large cupboard or container)
A press of books; of canvas; of clothes; of engagements; of people; of sail; of suspects.

PRIDE (a group, band or flock of animals)
A pride of lions; of peacocks.

PROCESSION (a group of moving people in an orderly state, *syn* cortège)

PROFUSION (abundance, a large number)
Profusion of commodities; of ideas; of promises.

PROMISE of tapsters (barmen, *collectively*)

PROUDSHOWING of tailors (15th century, tailors, *collectively*)

PROVISION of stewards (15th century, stewards, *collectively*)

PROVISIONS (store or stock prepared, eatables collected or stored)

PRUDENCE of vicars (vicars, *collectively*)

PSALTER of bishops (bishops, *collectively*)

PSITTOSIS of parrots (*collectively*, modern pun)

PUDDLING of mallard.

PUFF (a small quantity, emitted at a blast)
A puff of smoke; of vapour; of wind.

PUMMEL of masseurs (modern pun)

PURL of lace (a quantity of lace)

PYRAMID (any material thing or group of objects in the shape of a pyramid; also used figuratively)
Pyramid of bones; of books; of flame.

QUADRILLE (a meeting of four or more persons, *also* a band, troop or company)

QUARRY (a heap of deer killed at a hunt, *also* a heap of dead men)

QUATERNARY *or* **QUATERNION** (four things taken *collectively*, i.e., a group of four facts or circumstances)

QUAVER of coloraturas (modern)

QUEST (a body of persons appointed to hold an inquiry, *also* a collection or donation)
A quest of alms; of clerks (clerks, *collectively*); of cut-purses (thieves); of thoughts.

QUESTIONARY *or* **QUESTIONNAIRE** (collection of questions)

QUEUE (a line of persons or things)
A queue of carriages; of people.

QUICK (those who are alive, live plants, *collectively*, especially hawthorn)

QUILL (a roll of something resembling the shape of a quill)
A quill of cinnamon leaves; of dried bark.

QUINARY (set of five things)

QUINTETTE (any set of five, or things arranged for five, also a set of five people who play five-part music)

QUINTUPLET (a collection of five; five children born at the same labour)

QUIRE (a collection of 24 sheets of paper)

QUIVER (the sheath to carry arrows, hence the collection of arrows themselves)

QUODLIBET (a musical medley, a collection of several airs)

QUORUM (the number of members of a body or committee who together are competent to transact business, justices *collectively*, a select company)
A quorum of peers (two members of the House of Lords and the Lord Chancellor or his deputy)

QUOTITY (collection, group, a certain number of individuals)

RABBIN *or* **RABBINITE** (Rabbis, *collectively*, or as a class)

RABBITRY (a collection of hutches for tame rabbits)

RABBLE (pack, string, swarm of animals or insects, *syn* mob)
Rabble of bees; of books; of butterflies; of dishes; of doubts; of flies; of gnats; of insects; of licentious deities; of murderers; of passions; of pictures; of reasons; of remedies; of schoolmen; of strangers; of words.

RACE (a breed or class of individuals with common appearance, a company, *syn* herd, stud)
Race of birds; of doctors.

RACK (a rush or shock)
A rack of clouds (thin flying broken clouds); of wind (a sudden rush)

RACKET, *see* RAQUET.

RAFALE (burst of several rounds of artillery, *syn* fusillade)

RAFF (a promiscuous heap, jumble, a large quantity, a rabble, *syn* mob, riff-raff)
Raff of errors; of fellows.

RAFFLE (jangle or tangle, *syn* rubbish, tangle)
Raffle of cords; of flying drapery; of knaves; of spars.

RAFT (large collection of people or things taken indiscriminately, a dense flock of swimming birds, a collection of logs; fallen trees)
Raft of auks (at sea); of folk; of logs; of people; of reporters; of timber; of books.

RAFTER of turkeys.

RAG (colts, *collectively*)

RAGABASH (a rabble, riff-raff)

RAG-BAG (a motley collection)

RAG-TAG (the rabble or dregs of the community, *also* the whole amount, e.g., Rag, tag and bobtail)

RAGE (a violent passion, used as a collective noun in a few cases)
A rage of maidens (a passionate group); of teeth (when it feels as if all the teeth in the mouth ache)

RAIN (the falling or driving of numerous particles, *also* the particles themselves, *collectively*)
Rain of sparks.

RAISE (the things collected or levied, a heap of stones, *syn* cairn)

RAISIN (a bunch of grapes)

RAKE (collective term for colts or mules)

RAKEAGE (the collection of things made by raking or scouring)

RALLY (a group of persons gathered together with a common purpose, i.e., a political rally)

RAMAGE (branches, *collectively*)

RAMIFICATION (branches of a tree, *collectively*)

RANCHO (a Spanish term for a company who eat together, also a collection of huts)

RANGALE (rank and file, camp followers, *syn* herd)
Rangale of common herd of deer.

RANGE (a series of things, a row, line or file)
Range of beehives; of books; of buildings; of cliffs; of colours; of emotions; of hunters; of ladies; of mountains; of outbuildings; of pillars; of pipes; of pupils; of soldiers.

RANK (a row or line, series or tier, a social group)
Rank of taxi-cabs; of organ pipes; of soldiers.

RANT (fanatics, *collectively*)

RAQUET, RAQUETTE, RACQUET *or* **RACKET** (an assembly of high society at a private house, but usually a popular, noisy or confused group)

RASCAL (*collectively* the rabble, a mob, as of camp follower *or* lean ill-conditioned beast such as deer, *syn* rascality, rascaldry, rascalry, rascaldom)
Rascal of boys.

RASH (an unwelcome or unsightly outburst)
A rash of dermatologists (modern pun); of rain.

RAY (order or array of soldiers)

RAY, *see* BEAM.

REAM (a bale or bundle of clothes or paper, a large amount of paper)

REAP (reapers, *collectively*, *also* a handful or sheaf of grain)

RECESSION of economists (modern pun)

REGIMENT (a body of soldiers, *also* a large number of things)

RESERVOIR (a store, a collection, a reserve)

RESORT (people resorting or going together to a place, *syn* strong, concourse)
A resort of learned men.

RETINUE (a body of retainers, followers or attendants; *syn* servantry, staff)

REVELROUT (a lively crowd of revellers or merrymakers)

RHAPSODY (a collection of persons, notes, miscellaneous collections)
Rhapsody of condemned heresies; of errors and calumnies; of impertinence; of nations; of nonsense; of words.

RIBBON (a group or length of things in a form suggestive of a ribbon)

RICHESSE *or* **RICHNESS** (martins, *collectively*)

RICK (a heap or pile)
A rick of bricks; of coal; of grain; of snow.

RIFF-RAFF (a rabble, a mob, *also* refuse or rubbish)

RIGMAROLE (a succession of incoherent statements)
A rigmarole of nonsense.

RING (a circular arrangement or group, *syn* circle)
A ring of forts; of jewellers (modern pun); mushrooms.

RIOT (an unrestrained outburst)
A riot of laughter; of Romans; of words.

RIOTRY (rioters, *collectively*)

RIVER (figuratively an abundance) river of blood; of oil; of talk; of tears.

ROLL (a succession of sounds)
Roll of drum-beats; of thunder.

ROOKERY (a collection of rooks' nests, breeding place or large colony of seabirds or other marine mammals, breeding place, hence a group of gregarious birds such as heron or penguins, *also* a cluster of dilapidated buildings, *syn* building)
Rookery of albatrosses; of herons; of penguins; of prostitutes; of rooks; of seals; of volcanoes.

ROOST (a collection of fowls roosting together)

ROPE (a row or string of items or people)
Rope of onions; of pearls.

ROSARY (a bed of roses, a string of beads, a chaplet or garland or collection of poems or quotations)
Rosary of good works; of prayers; of quotations; of roses.

ROSTER (roll or list)
Roster of honours.

ROT (a file of six soldiers)

ROULEAU (roll of coins)

ROUND (a circle, a group or series of events)
Round of applause; of drinks; of duties; of knowledge; of pleasures; of politicians; of toasts; of visits.

ROUT *or* **ROUTE** (a troop, throng, company)
Rout of knights; of snails; of soldiers; of wolves; of words and actions; of gentlemen.

RUCK (a large number, a crowd, a heap or pile)
Ruck of coal; of horses; of stones.

RUELLE (an 18th century morning social gathering in the bedroom of a fashionable lady)

RUMBLE of bases (modern pun)

RUN (assemblage or school of fish which migrate)
Run of salmon; of whales; of fish.

RUSH (a group formed by a moving forward with great speed)
A rush of dunbirds; of troops; of water; of wind.

SAFE of ducks.

SAFEGUARD of porters (15th century)

SAILFUL of wind.

SAILRIFE (full of sailing ships)

SALON (a gathering or reception in a Parisian house)

SALVO (a salute or discharge of firearms, rockets, etc., shouts or cheers of the crowd)
Salvo of applause; of gunfire; of rockets; of confetti; salvos of despair.

SAMPLE of salesmen (modern)

SAVAGEDOM (savage people, *collectively*)

SAVAGERY (savage beasts or savages, *collectively*)

SAWT of lions (French for leap)

SCAFF-RAFF (rabble, riff-raff, *Scottish*)

SCAFFOLDING of words.

SCANTLING (a small portion, a spare amount)

SCATTERING (sparse amount or number, *syn* scantling)
Scattering of learning; of thoughts.

SCHEDULE (written or printed formal list, hence often the items listed)
Schedule of documents.

SCHOOL (body of pupils in a school, a group of painters or musicians; the disciples of a teacher, a collective body of teachers; company of thieves; set of persons who agree on certain philosophical, scientific or other opinions, *also* a herd of sea mammals or fish)
School of beggars; of card players; of clerks; of dolphins; of fish; of gulls; of herrings; of hippopotami; of a troop of the Imperial Guard; of painters; of pamphlets; of pheasants; of pick-pockets; of pilchards; of porpoises; of thieves; of whales.

SCOLDING of kempsters (15th century, seamstresses)

SCOOP (an amount of something obtained in large quantity as if with a scoop)

SCORE (group or set of twenty, often approximate)
Score of miles; of people.

SCOTSHIP (a party or group paying 'scot and lot', a communal fine or tax)

SCOURGE (a load or burden)
A scourge of mosquitoes; of priests; of Turks.

SCRAP (a bit *or* fragment)
A scrap of evidence; of learning; of news.

SCREECH of gulls.

SCREED (lengthy discourse, harangue)
Screed of doctrine; of malevolence; of notes; of poetry (long tirade)

SCRY (flock of wild fowl; a shouting clamorous group)

SEA (anything resembling the seas in vastness, a great quantity, a flood)
Sea of acclamations; of blood; of carpets; of clouds; of discussion; of examples; of forces and passions; of glory; of heads; of troubles; of wrath.

SEAM (a horse-load, varying according to commodity, but specifically 8 bushels of grain)
Seam of glass (120 lb.); of grain (8 bushels); of sand (6–8 pecks); of apples (9 pecks).

SECT (people following a particular creed or set of opinions)
Sect of philosophers; of writers.

SEDGE (collection of rush-like marsh plants; group of sea or marsh birds, *also* sege or siege)
Sedge of bitterns; of cranes; of herons.

SEETHE of patriotic feelings.

SELECTION (collection of things selected)

SENTENCE of judges (15th century)

SEPT (clan or tribe)

SERIAL (an arrangement of items in a series, *syn* sequence, rank or row)

SERIES (a number of things or events connected by some like relationship, *syn* chain)
Series of calamities; of triumphs; of revolutions.

SERGE of herons, *see also* SEDGE.

SERON (a bale or package of exotic spices or commodities)

SERRY (a crowd or press of people)

SERVANTRY (a body of servants)

SERVICE (a set or number of articles, *collectively*)
Services of china; of plate; of tableware.

SESSION (a group of judges, administrators or other persons in session)

SET (a number of items of similar nature usually used together, *syn* clique, party, gang)

Set of bowls; of chairs; of china; of eggs; of games; of oysters (the crop of young oysters in any locality); of ushers.

SHAFT of sunlight.

SHEAF (collection of things bound together, a large bundle, cluster of flowers, leaves, *plural* sheaves, *syn* garb, gavel) Sheaf of arrows (24); of banners; of beans; of blooms; of corn; of grain; of hemp; of jets of flame; of jets of water; of librarians; of lines (geometry); of rye; of timber; of letters; of rain; of rays (light rays).

SHELTRON (band, army, battalion or squadron)

SHELVING (shelves, *collectively*)

SHIVE *or* **SHOVE** (fragments, *collectively*, or specifically the woody part of flax which breaks, a cluster of splinters of raw fibres in paper making, *syn* brash)

SHIVOO (social gathering, *Australian*)

SHOAL (great number, crowd, throng, *especially* of fish) Shoal of fish; of herrings; of letters; of pilchards; of people; of troubles; of minnows; of perch; of sticklebacks.

SHOCK (pile or assemblage of sheaves of grain, wheat, rye, etc., a heap, bunch or bundle of things, a crowd of people) A shock of folk; of actors; of hair.

SHOT (pellets, *collectively*) of fish (single draught or catch of fish); of foot soldiers (soldiers with firearms); of nets (entire throw of nets at one time).

SHOTE (a clump, a group)

SHOVE, *see* SHIVE.

SHOWER (resembling a fall of rain, a copious supply, an uncomplimentary term referring to a crowd of people) Shower of blows; of blessings; of bullets; of gifts; of meteorologists; of rain; of sleet, of snow; of sparks.

SHREWDNESS (apes, *collectively*)

SHRIVEL of critics.

SHRUBBERY (shrubs, *collectively*)

SIEGE (a flock)
Siege of bitterns; of cranes; of herons.

SIGHT (a great number, a quantity or sum)
A sight of lawyers; of money.

SIGNARY (a series or arrangement of signs)
Signary of signs, hieroglyphs or other alphabetical signs.

SINGULAR (a pack of boars)

SITTING (the meeting together of a body of persons authorized to transact business, the number of eggs covered by a fowl in a single brooding, a number of people taking a meal, or sitting an examination at a certain time)
Sitting of a commission; of judicial court; of Parliament.

SKEIN (a flight of wild fowl, duck or geese; a quantity of yarn thread or silk taken from the reel)

SKELP (a heavy fall of rain)

SKILL (those in a profession or occupation considered *collectively*, a guild or craft)

SKIRL of piper.

SKULK (a furtive group)
A skulk of foxes; of friars; of thieves.

SKULL (a school or shoal of fish, *obsolete*)

SKY of pictures (the top row of paintings in an exhibition gallery)

SLASH (a large quantity of liquid, e.g., soup or broth)

SLATE (a list of candidates prepared for nomination)
Slate of candidates; of officers; of horses (in a race)

SLATHER (a large quantity)

SLEUTH, SLEWTHE, SLOTH, SLOUGHT (a flock, mass, a company of bears)

SLEW *or* **SLUE** (a large quantity, a lot)
A slew of people.

SLOUCH of models (modern pun)

SLUMBER of the Old Guard.

SMACK (a smattering, a small quantity)
A smack of knowledge; of wit; of jellyfish.

SMALL BEER (any collection of trifles or trifling matters)

SMERE *or* **SMEAR** (punning terms)
Smere of courtiers; a smear of gynaecologists.

SMUTH of jellyfish.

SNEER of butlers.

SODALITY (a fellowship or fraternity)

SORD (a flock of mallard); of ducks (*also* sore or safe)

SORT *or* **SORTE** (a group having similar features, a group of people or animals, a crowd or flock, *syn* set *or* suit, batch)
A sort of figs; of raisins; of traitors.

SOUNDER (a herd of wild swine, pigs or boars)

SOWNDER of swans.

SOWSE of lions (*used in Egerton MSS*)

SPAN of mules.

SPANGE of stars.

SPECIES (a group of individuals of common parentage, a sort, kind or variety)

SPILING (piles, *collectively*)

SPRAY (a group of small branches and foliage, anything resembling this, *syn* cascade)
Spray of branches; of flowers; of water.

SPREAD (food, *collectively*)

SPRING (a group of animals or birds flushed from their covert)
Spring of teal.

SPRINKLING (a small quantity falling in scattering drops; a small number scattered here and there)
A sprinkling of people; of pepper; of rain.

SPURT (a sudden violent outbreak, as of feeling or energy, a violent gushing of liquids)
A spurt of water.

SQUAD (a small number of individuals engaged in a common task or occupation)
Squad of beaters; of soldiers.

SQUADRON (any body of men in regular formation, a division of the fleet or air force, in the army it is a force of 150–200 men)
Squadron of aircraft; of angels; of ships.

SQUARE (a body of troops drawn up in a square to repel the enemy)

SQUAT of daubers (15th century plasterers)

SQUIRY *or* **SQUIRARCHY** (a company of squires)

STABLE (horses, *collectively*)

STACK (a large quantity, a group or set, an orderly pile or heap, bookstacks, *collectively*, *also* a unit of measure of coal or fuel (4 cubic yards), a stack of arms (rifles stacked in a pyramid)
Stack of billets; of bills; of books; of letters; of money.

STAFF (a body of servants, officers, nurses or employees, *collectively*)

STALK of foresters (foresters, *collectively*)

STAND (a suit or set, e.g., as of soldiers, clothes, a suit of armour, a hive of bees, *syn* set)
Stand of plovers; of flamingoes.

STANZA (a group of lines of verse)

STARE of owls (modern, a group of owls)

STATE of princes (princes, *collectively*)

STATUARY (statues, *collectively*)

STONE of drunks (modern)

STOOK (a heap or bundle or truss of flax or of sheaves of grain)

STORE (an accumulation of material)
Store of knowledge; of provisions.

STORM (shower or flight of objects, *also* a passionate outburst)
Storm of arrows; of sobs; of wrath.

STRAIN (a family of people or animals, a group of plants bred away from the original species)

STREAM (a continuous flow)
Streams of abuse; of beneficence; of cold air; of emigrants; of ice (when the pieces are long and narrow); of people; of words.

STRENGTH (a body of soldiers)

STRIKE (a dry measure varying from 2 pecks to 4 bushels, now obsolete)
Strike of flax.

STRING (a line or series of things or animals arranged in a line, or continuous one after the other)
A string of arguments; of beads; of excuses; of lies; of oaths; of onions; of pearls; of ponies; of racehorses; of sausages; of violinists (modern pun)

STUBBORNNESS of rhinoceros.

STUCK of jellyfish.

STUD (a collection of horses or other animals kept for breeding, racing or riding, *syn* stable, string)
Stud of dogs; of horses; of mares; of racehorses; of poker players.

SUBTLETY of sergeants (15th century, arises from the use of the title sergeant for lawyers, hence it becomes lawyers, *collectively*)

SUCCESSION (a series of things)
A succession of facts; of heirs.

SUCCOUR of galleys (ships, *collectively*, a galley could be either a low vessel rowed by slaves *or* a large row-boat used by customs officers or by press gangs)

SUIT (a number of things used together, *syn* set, stand)
Suit of armour; of cards; of clothes.

SUITE (a connected series of items, *also* a retinue of attendants, *syn* staff, set)
Suite of minerals; of rooms or apartments.

SUM (a quantity of money, of numbers, a host, an assembly)

SUPERFLUITY of nuns (15th century)

SWARM (a large number of small animals, usually in motion, *also* applied to people or things, *syn* bike, flock)
Swarm of ants; of bees; of eels; of fanatic monks; of flies; of gnats; of hornets; of insects; of meteorites; of wasps.

SWISH of hairdressers (modern pun)

SYNOD (an assembly of clergy, ministers or elders)
Synod of prelates.

SYNTAX (a connected system or order, a union of things)

SYSTEM (an assembly of objects arranged in a series of subordinates which conform to a laid-down method)
System of botany; of communications; of philosophy; of railways.

TABERNACLE of bakers.

TALE (a number of things; a list or series)

TALENT (an abundance or plenty, *collectively* persons of ability or skill, or habitual gamblers, *also* girls)

TANGLE (a knot of threads or other items in confused piles, also used figuratively)

TASS (a heap or pile)

TEAM (a group or brood of animals, animals moving together, animals harnessed together, persons joined together in some sporting, commercial, competitive or other activity)
A team of athletes; of carriage horses; of debaters; of dolphins; of ducks; of footballers; of oxen; of polo horses; of swans.

TEEM (brood of young ducks, from Anglo-Saxon)

TEMPERANCE of cooks (15th century)

TEMPLARY (Knights Templar, *collectively*)

TEMPLE (a local group of Oddfellows)

TENANTRY (a body of tenants)

TERRACE (a raised surface or platform, a series of things, especially houses)

THESAURUS (a treasury or storehouse, therefore a repository, as of words, i.e., Roget's Thesaurus)

THOUGH of barons.

THRAVE of threshers (from the use of the word as a bundle, a sheaf, a crowd or throng, *also* specifically 24 sheaves of corn)

THREAT (a crowd, press, or troop)

THRONG (a large number of people, *syn* multitude)

THRUST (a large milling crowd)

TIDE (a stream, a current of things or emotions)
Tide of blood; of feeling; of events.

TIDING of magpies (a flock)

TIERCE (a third part of a thing or group)

TIMBER of skins (40 skins of martens, ermines and sables, *or* 120 skins of other animals)

TISSUE (a web, a texture, a framework)
A tissue of lies; of misfortunes.

TITTERING of magpies (a flock)

TOFT (a small group of trees)

TOGGERY *or* **TOGS** (clothes, *collectively*)

TOK (nesting place or assembly)
Tok of caper cailzes (great grouse)

TOKEN (a small amount)
A token of paper (250 printed impressions)

TORRENT (a violent or rapid flood)
Torrent of eloquence; of oaths; of vices; of words.

TOWER (a group of towering items)
Tower of giraffes.

TRACE of hares (referring to marks in the snow)

TRAIN (a number of followers, a procession, a company in order, a succession of connected objects or ideas)
A camel train; a funeral train; train of courtiers; of happy sentiments; of thoughts; of words.

TRANCE of lovers (modern)

TREASURY (collection of wit, of poems or quotations)

TRESS (a plait, braid or lock)
Tress of flowers; of hair; of straw.

TRIAD (a group of three)
Triad of dieties.

TRIBE (a social group consisting of a number of families, any group having a common feature)
Tribe of goats; of savages; of sparrows.

TRIBUTE (a sum of money or valuables paid by one to another, a personal contribution of praise)
Tribute of affection; of tears.

TRINE (a triad, three, trinity, *also* a favourable aspect of planets)
A trine of astrologers; a single trine of brass tortoises.

TRINKET of corvisors (shoemakers, *collectively*, 15th century)

TRINKETRY (trinkets, *collectively*)

TRIP (a flock or troop, a brood or litter)
Trip of dottrel; of goats (also trippe); of hares; of hippies; of stoats; of wild fowl; of swine; of sheep.

TRIPLETRINE (the nine muses)

TRIUMVIRATE (a group, party, or association of three)

TROOP *or* **TROUPE** (a collection of people; a company; a number of things; soldiers, *collectively*, a company of actors, *syn* band, party)

Troop of acrobats; of actors; of baboons; of dancers; of kangaroos; of minstrels; of monkeys; of players; of soldiers; of tenements; of dogfish; of lions.

TRUSS (bundle, pack or package)
Truss of hay (60 lb. new hay; 56 lb. old hay); of straw (36 lb.); of trifles.

TRUST (a group of people appointed as trustees)

TUBING (tubes, *collectively*)

TUFT (a small cluster, *syn* bavin, bunch)
Tuft of feathers; of grass; of hairs; of plants.

TUMBLE (confused pile or mass, *syn* jumble, tangle)

TUMULT (violent commotion)
Tumult of passions; of spirits.

TURMOIL of porpoises.

TURN of turtles.

TUSSOCK (a tuft, a small cluster)
A tussock of grass; of hair; of twigs.

UNCTION of undertakers (modern)

UNEMPLOYMENT of graduates (modern)

UNHAPPINESS of husbands (modern)

UNKINDNESS of ravens (15th century)

UNTRUTH of sompners (*variant* of somner, *or* summoner (15th century))

VAGABONDAGE (vagabonds, *collectively*)

VAN (a company or troops moving forward, frequently used in a military sense referring to a forward section of the force)

VARIETY (a number or collection of different things, *syn* miscellany)

VARLETRY (varlets, *collectively*)

VASSALAGE (vassals, *collectively*)

VERBIAGE of words (a large number or over-use of words)

VESTRY (Church of England, the body which administers the affairs of the church or parish)

VOLERY (a flight or flock of birds)

VOLLEY (a flight of missiles, a burst of many things at one time)
Volley of arrows; of bullets; of grievances; of gunfire; of oaths; of words.

WAD (a little mass, a tuft or bundle)
Wad of hay; of money; of tobacco; of tow.

WALE (a selection, or that chosen as the best)

WALK (a procession, hence the group in the procession)
A walk of snails; of snipe.

WANDERING of tinkers (tinkers, *collectively*)

WAP (a bundle or truss of straw)

WARD (a body of people guarding or defending, such as a garrison, its use survives with ward-room)

WARP (a throw or cast, a set of four)
A warp of herrings; of oysters.

WARREN (a place granted by the King for keeping certain animals, hares, conies, partridge, pheasants, *also* a place in the river for keeping fish) a rabbit warren.

WATCH (a body of watchmen or guards, *also* a flock, i.e., a watch of nightingales)

WAVE (a body of water, something resembling the same)
A wave of admirals; of emotion; of enthusiasm.

WAYWARDNESS of haywards (a hayward is a parish official in charge of fences and enclosures, *also* a waywardness of herdsmen)

WEALTH (a large possession, a great amount)
A wealth of feeling; of information; of knowledge; of learning.

WEB (a texture, a fabrication, system, *syn* tissue)
Web of conjecture; of lies.

WEDGE (anything in the form of a wedge, e.g., a body of troops, also used for a wedge of swans)

WEIGHT of opinion (an unidentified group)

WELL (a source of supply)
Well of mercy; of serious thought.

WELTER (confusion or turmoil)
Welter of controversies; of opinions.

WERE, WERED *or* **WERING** (a military force, a band of troops)

WHACK (a portion or share)
Whack of spoils; of troubles.

WHARFAGE (wharves, *collectively*)

WHEEN (a division, group, a small amount)

WHINE of clarinettists (modern)

WHISK (a small bunch of grass, straw, etc., *syn* tuft)

WHISP (a flock of snipe, *also* wisp)

WINCE of dentists (modern)

WING (a flock of plovers)

WISP, *see* WHISP.

WITENAGEMOT (an assembly *or* council of the Witan – the Anglo-Saxon Council to the King)

WOBBLE of cyclists (modern)

WOMENHOOD (women, *collectively*)

WOOD CHOIR (a chorus of birds)

WORSHIP of writers (authors, *collectively*)

WRANGLE of philosophers (modern)

WREATH (a garland *or* intertwined chaplet and anything resembling it; *also* a drift, as of snow or sand) a wreath of flowers; of smoke.

YEOMANRY (yeomen, *collectively*, *also* volunteer force)

YIELD (an amount or quantity yielded or grown, i.e., a yield of fruit)

YOKE of oxen.

ZEAL of zebras.

ZODIAC (a set of twelve)

ZOO (a collection of animals)

Part 2

Dictionary of Subjects

ABUSE, *see* OATHS.

ACADEMICS—a calendar of academics; a flight of academics, *see also* GRADUATES, GRAMMARIANS, KNOWLEDGE, TEACHERS.

ACCIDENTS—a chapter *or* succession of accidents.

ACCLAMATION—a sea of acclamations, *see also* PRAISE.

ACCOUNTANTS—a column of accountants.

ACCOUNTS—a divan (a register of accounts)

ACQUAINTANCES—a circle *or* cohort of acquaintances *see also* FRIENDS.

ACROBATS—a troupe of acrobats.

ACTORS—a cast, chorus (Greek), company or condescension of actors; a cry of players; an entrance of actresses; a troupe (actors, *collectively*); a shock of actors.

ADMIRALS—a wave of admirals.

ADMIRERS—a clique *or* circle of admirers; a claque (in France a group of paid applauders)

ADVERSITY—a scourge of adversity.

ADVERTISEMENTS—a crowd of advertisements.

ADVISERS—a camarilla (a group of secret advisers)

ADVOCATES—a faculty of advocates, *see also* LAWYERS.

AFFAIRS—an olio of romantic affairs.

AFFECTIONS—a flock of affections; a tribute of affection; a chaplet of domestic affections.

AIR—a stream *or* body of cold air; a pocket or pillar of air.

AIRCRAFT—an armada, fleet, or squadron of aircraft; *or* airfleet, flight (i.e., aircraft, *collectively*)

AIRMEN—crew *or* flight of airmen; flush of Wing Commanders.

ALBATROSS—a rookery.

ALDERMEN—a bench or guzzle of aldermen.

ALE—a dozen of ale (twelve pots of ale)

ALLEGATIONS—a camp of allegations.

ALLEYS—a nest of alleys.

ALMS—a quest of alms.

AMMUNITION—a shot (pellets, *collectively*)

ANATOMISTS—a corps of anatomists.

ANECDOTES—a conglomerate of anecdotes.

ANGELS—a bevy of maids of heaven; a bunch of cherubs; a choir of angels; a concert, flight, host *or* legion of angels; a minstrelsy of heaven; a squadron of angels; heavenry or heavenware (angels, *collectively*); a phantasmagoria of contending angels; a power of angels.

ANGER—accumulation of ire; gusts of temper; storms of wrath.

ANIMALS (there are a number of general terms, e.g., flock, flight, herd or drove, also see under individual names of animals)—centeener (a large number of animals having a common parentage); menagerie or zoo (wild or tame animals, *collectively*); tribe or cluster.

ANTELOPES—a herd of antelopes.

ANTS—an army, bike, colony or swarm of ants.

APARTMENTS—a suite of apartments.

APES—a shrewdness of apes.

APOSTLES—a company, congregation, convent *or* fellowship of apostles.

APPLAUSE—a burst of applause; a claque (group of applauders); a hand (a round of applause); a round or salvo of applause.

APPLES—pot of apples (five pecks); seam of apples (nine pecks)

APPREHENSIONS—a gale of doubts and apprehensions.

ARCHDEACONS—a bundle of archdeacons, *see also* CLERGY.

ARCHERS—an archery (archers, *collectively*)

ARGUMENTS—an army or camp of arguments; a forest of verbal arguments; a host, nest, platoon *or* string of arguments.

ARMOUR—an armoury (armour, *collectively*); a cast, stand or suit of armour.

ARMS—a pile of arms; a stack (three or more rifles stacked in a pyramid); a stand of arms (complete set of arms for one soldier); *also* ARMOURY.

ARROWS—a cloud, sheaf, storm, quiver *or* volley of arrows.

ARTICLES—a posse of articles (literary).

ARTILLERY—a peal of artillery; a rafale (a burst of severe or heavy rounds)

ARTISTS—a cabal, colony or school of artists, *see also* Painters.

ASHES—a bed of ashes; a cascade of volcanic ash.

ASSES—a pace *or* herd of asses; a drove of asses.

ASSOCIATIONS—a confluence of associations (historical links with a place or person)

ASTROLOGERS—a trine of astrologers; a knot of astrologers.

ASTRONOMERS—a galaxy of astronomers.

ATHLETES—a team of athletes.

ATOMS—a conjugation of atoms.

ATTENDANTS—suite *or* train of attendants *or* servants; meiny, port *or* retinue (attendants *or* servants, *collectively*)

ATTORNEYS—array of attorneys, *see also* Lawyers.

ATTRIBUTES—a herd of attributes.

AUKS—a colony of auks (on land); a flock *or* raft of auks (at sea).

AUTHORS—a consort *or* fry of authors, *see also* Writers.

AVOCETS—a colony of avocets.

BABOONS—a troop of baboons.

BACHELORS—a debauching *or* parcel of bachelors; bachelry (bachelors, *collectively*)

BACON—a side of bacon; a lock of bacon (a small amount)

BADGERS—a cete *or* colony of badgers; a set of badgers.

BAKERS—an aroma of bakers; a tabernacle of bakers.

BALLADS—congeries *or* garlands of ballads, *see also* POEMS.

BALUSTERS—balustrade.

BANANAS—a bunch *or* hand of bananas.

BANDERILLEROS—a leap of banderilleros.

BANDITS—banditti (bandits, *collectively*), *see also* BRIGANDS, ROBBERS, THIEVES.

BANDSMEN—a furore of bandsmen.

BANKNOTES—a flood *or* wad of banknotes, *see also* MONEY.

BANNERS—a festoon *or* sheaf of banners.

BARBARIANS—a horde of barbarians.

BARBERS—a babble of barbers.

BARFLIES—a buzz of barflies.

BARK—a quill of dried bark (a roll of something which resembles a quill)

BARONS—Baronage *or* Baroney (*collectively*)

BARTENDERS—a blarney of bartenders.

BARRIERS—a line of barriers.

BARRISTERS—a mess of judges and barristers; the bar (barristers and lawyers, *collectively*), *see also* JUDGES, LAWYERS.

BARS—barring (decorative bars or stripes, *collectively*)

BASEBALL TEAM—a nine (the players, *collectively*)

BASES (musical instruments or voices)—a rumble of bases.

BATS—a colony of bats.

BAYONETS—a grove of bayonets.

BEACONS—beaconage (beacons, *collectively*)

BEADS—a chaplet or string of beads; a rosary.

BEANS—a mess *or* sheaf of beans.

BEARS—a sleuthe, slewthe, sloth *or* slought of bears.

BEATERS (game-beaters)—a squad of beaters.

BEAUTIES (girls)—a bevy of beauties, *see also* GIRLS.

BEAVERS—a lodge of beavers.

BEER—a dozen of beer (twelve pots); a crate of beer.

BEES—a bike of wild bees; a cluster of bees (around the queen); a cast of bees (an afterswarm); a college, colony, a drift, an erst, game, grist, hive of bees; a fry (a swarm of young bees); a peck of bees (enough to fill a peck); a rabble, stand *or* swarm of bees; *also* a range of bee hives.

BEGGARS—a fighting of beggars; a school of beggars; beggary (beggars, *collectively*)

BELIEF—an accrescence of belief.

BELLS—a change, chime *or* peal of bells.

BELTS—belting (belts, *collectively*)

BENEFICENCE—a stream of beneficence.

BILLETS (of wood)—a stack of billets.

BILLS—a stack of bills (accounts); a sheaf of bills (paper money)

BIRDS—a battery, cast, a congregation, covert or covey, dissimulation, drift, flight, fleet, flock, flurry, flush (game birds disturbed), nest, nide, party, pod, race, raff, spring (game birds flushed) or birds; an aviary; a volery; a woodchoir (chorus of birds in the wood); a consort of bird calls.

BISHOPS—a bench, brace (two), consistory, or conventicle of bishops; a bishopdom (bishops, *collectively*); episcopate (the body of bishops); a psalter of bishops, *see also* CLERGY.

BISON—a herd of bison.

BITTERNS—a flock, sedge, sege or siege of bitterns.

BLACKFISH—a grind of blackfish.

BLESSINGS—a shower of blessings.

BLOCKHEADS—a parcel of blockheads.

BLOOD—a pool, sea *or* tide of blood.

BLOODHOUNDS—a sute of bloodhounds.

BLOOMS—a sheaf of blooms, *see also* FLOWERS.

BLOWS—a battery *or* shower of blows.

BLUNDERS—a cento *or* succession of blunders.

BOARS—a singular *or* sounder of boars; a herd, *see also* PIGS, SWINE.

BOATS, *see* SHIPS.

BODIES—a carnage of carcasses; a quarry (a heap of dead men *or* animals)

BOILERS, *see* HENS.

BONDS—a block of bonds or shares.

BONDSMEN—a helotry (bondsmen, *collectively*)

BONES—a pile *or* pyramid of bones.

BOOKS—a concourse, corpus, host, mob (Australian), pack, press, pyramid, rabble, raft, range, selection *or* stack of books; edition (all those books printed at one time, not to be confused with an impression); impression (a reprint of an edition without any alterations); a library (a collection of books, *collectively*); bibliography.

BORES—boredom (bores, *collectively*)

BOTANY—a system of botany classifications.

BOTTLERS—a draft of bottlers.

BOTTLES—a cellar (wine bottles, *collectively*)

BOUGHS—a bow *or* boughpot, *see also* BRANCHES.

BOWLS—a set of bowls.

BOXES—a nest of boxes.

BOYS—blush, crop, gang, leer of boys; boyhood (boys, *collectively*); a rascal of boys.

BRACKETS—bracketing (brackets, *collectively*)

BRANCHES—a spray of branches; branching, frondage, ramage, ramification (all terms for branches, *collectively*)

BRATS—a passel of brats.

BRAVERY—a mint of bravery.

BREAD—a cast, batch *or* dozen of bread.

BREWERS—a feast of brewers (15th century)

BRICKS—a clam, clamp *or* rick of bricks.

BRIDGE (cards)—a hand (a group of players)

BRIEFS (legal)—a boredom of briefs.

BRIGANDS—brigandage (brigands, *collectively*), *see also* BANDITS.

BROKERS—a portfolio of brokers.

BROOKS—a meinie of brooks.

BROTH—a slash of broth.

BRUISES—a mass of bruises.

BRUSHWOOD—a bavin (or bundle) of brushwood.

BRUTES—a parcel of brutes.

BUCKETS—a chain of buckets.

BUCKS—a brace (two), a leash (three) of bucks, *see also* DEER.

BUFFALO—a gang, herd *or* obstinacy of buffalo.

BUILDINGS—a complex *or* range of buildings.

BULLFINCHES—a bellowing of bullfinches.

BULLETS—a fusillade, hail, shower *or* volley of bullets.

BULLOCKS—a drove of bullocks.

BULLS (papal documents)—a bullary (bulls, *collectively*)

BUNGLES—a concatenation of bungles and contradictions.

BURGESSES—a good advice of burgesses.

BUSES—a fleet *or* lurch of buses.

BUSHES—bush (bushes, *collectively*); frondage (bushes, *collectively*); a nest of low bushes.

BUSTARDS—a flock of bustards.

BUTCHERS—a goring of butchers (15th century)

BUTLERS—a draught *or* sneer of butlers, *see also* SERVANTS, WAITERS.

BUTTER—a pot of butter (originally 14 lb.); a pat of butter (a small amount)

BUTTERFLIES—a rabble of butterflies.

CABS—a rank of cabs.

CALAMITIES—a series of calamities.

CALICO—a piece of calico (10 yards)

CALUMNIES—a bundle of calumnies; a rhapsody of errors and calumnies.

CAMELS—a herd of camels; a caravan (camels with merchandise, *collectively*); a train (a camel train); a flock.

CAMP FOLLOWERS—a rangale.

CAMPERS—a camp (campers, *collectively*)

CANALS—a flight of locks; a network of canals.

CANDIDATES (political)—a slate of candidates.

CANNONS (armaments)—cannonry (cannons, *collectively*)

CANONS (ecclesiastical)—a chapter, college *or* dignity of canons, *see also* CLERGY.

CANVAS—a bolt of canvas (40 yards)

CANVAS (sails)—a press of canvas.

CAPER CAILZES (giant grouse)—a tok of caper cailzes.

CAPONS—mews (*collectively* hens or capons fattening)

CARCASSES—a carnage of carcasses.

CARDINALS—a college, conclave *or* congregation of cardinals; cardinalate (cardinals, *collectively*), *see also* CLERGY.

CARDIOLOGISTS—a flutter of cardiologists.

CARDS—a castle, deck, flush, hand, monte (or monty), pack *or* suit of cards; a school of cardplayers.

CARES—a multitude of cares.

CARIBOU—a herd of caribou.

CARPETS—a sea *or* pile of carpets.

CARRIAGES—a cavalcade or queue of carriages.

CARS—a fleet or procession of cars; a draft of cars (used for special duties); a motorcade (a group of cars in procession)

CARTERS—a lash of carters (15th century)

CARTWHEELS—a gang of cartwheels (a set)

CARVERS—an embracing of carvers (15th century)

CASTLES—a heap of castles; an agglomeration of turrets.

CATERPILLARS—an army *or* nest of caterpillars.

CATHOLICS—a consult of catholics, *see also* PAPISTS.

CATS—a clowder *or* clutter of cats; a destruction of wild cats; a dout of wild cats; a glaring of cats, *see also* KITTENS.

CATTLE—a bow, bunch, creaght, draft, drift, drive, drove, flote, head, herd *or* lot of cattle; a booly (a company of herdsmen wandering with their cattle); a dairy (milch cows)

CAUSES—a concatenation of causes and effects.

CAVALRY—cavalry (horses and horsemen, *collectively*); a cavalcade of horsemen; a cornet of horse; a body of horse, *see also* HORSES.

CELLARS—cellarage (cellars, *collectively*)

CHAIRS—a set *or* stack of chairs.

CHAMOIS—a herd of chamois.

CHAMPIONS—a cycle of champions.

CHANCES—a conglomeration *or* huddle of chances.

CHANGES—a cycle of changes.

CHARIOTEERS—a chariotry (charioteers, *collectively*)

CHARTERS—a chartulary (charters, *collectively*)

CHERUBS—a bunch of cherubs, cherubim (cherubs, *collectively*)

CHESSMEN—a meiny of chessmen (a set)

CHICKEN—a brood, cletch, clutch, hatching, nest, parcel, peep, pepe of chicken, *see also* HENS.

CHILDREN—an aerie, brood, creche *or* ingratitude of children; a horde of urchins; a mess of sons; a passel of brats.

CHINA—a service *or* set of china; crockery (china or earthenware, *collectively*)

CHINCHILLA—a colony of chinchilla.

CHORISTERS—a choir *or* chapel of choristers.

CHOUGHS—a chattering of choughs; a clattering of choughs.

CHRISTIANS—flock *or* fold of Christians; a communion *or* denomination (both *collectively*)

CHRONOGRAPHERS—a gang of chronographers.

CHURCH PEWS—pewage *or* pewing (used *collectively*)

CHURCHES—a cluster of churches.

CHURLS—a cluster of churls.

CINEMA-GOERS—an optience.

CINNAMON LEAVES—a quill of cinnamon (a roll resembling a quill)

CIRCUMSTANCES—a chain *or* conjuncture of circumstances, *see also* EVENTS.

CITATIONS—a clutter of citations.

CLAMS—a bed of clams.

CLAMOURS—a confusion of clamours.

CLARINETTISTS—a whine of clarinettists.

CLERGY—an abominable sight of monks; an assembly of clergy; a bench of Bishops; Bishopdom (bishops, *collectively*); a body of divinity (clergy, *collectively*); a brace of Bishops; a bunch of Patriarchs; a bundle of Archdeacons; a canon of monastic rule; the calling (the ministry itself); cardinalate; a cell (a small religious group); cenoby of monks; chantry of priests; chapelry; chapter of canons or friars; charge of curates; clerkage or clerkery (holy clerks, i.e., clergy); the Cloth (in phrases as 'respect for the cloth'); college of canons *or* Cardinals; a communion (a sect of part of a church); a community of monks; a conclave of Cardinals; a cone of Prelacy; a confession (a sect or part of the church); a congregation of Cardinals *or* monasteries; a consistory of Bishops; a consult of Jesuits; convents of nuns, friars or monks; conventicle of Bishops; converting of preachers; convocation of clergy; decanter of Deans; decorum of Deans; dignity of canons; discretion of priests; flap of nuns; friarty *or* friary (friars, *collectively*); mass of priests; the ministry; monkery, monkhood *or* monkship (monks, *collectively*); nunnery (nuns, *collectively*); an observance of hermits; an observancy (a community of monks following a rule); a phyle (a group of Greek priests); Pontificate; Prelacy (prelates, *collectively*; prudence of vicars; scourge of priests; skulk of friars; superfluity of nuns; swarm of fanatical monks; synod of Prelates.

CLERKS—a gang, quest *or* school of clerks; a clerkage *or* clerkery (clerks, *collectively*)

CLIENTS—clientele (clients, *collectively*)

CLIFFS—an array, palisade *or* range of cliffs.

CLOTH—a piece of cloth (10 yds.); a bolt of cloth (40 yds.)

CLOTHES—a bundle, outfit, press (i.e., wardrobe), ream (bundle *or* bale of clothes *or* paper), stand *or* suit of clothes, clothing, finery, gear *or* toggery (all used *collectively*); a layette (babies clothes); and lingerie (underclothes, *collectively*)

CLOUDS—a bank, canopy, field, flight, pillar, rack *or* sea of clouds; a brewing of black clouds.

CLOVER—a lock of clover (a small amount)

CLUBS (social)—a knot of clubs.

COAL—a bed, pack (3 bushels), pie, rick, ruck, seam *or* stock (4 cubic yards) of coal.

COBBLERS—a cutting of cobblers; a drunkenship of cobblers (15th century), *see also* SHOEMAKERS.

COBWEBS—a festoon of cobwebs.

COCKLES—a bed of cockles.

COCKROACHES—an intrusion of cockroaches.

COD—a lap of cod.

COINS—a hoard of coins; a journey (a batch of coins minted together, specifically 720 oz. *or* 2,000 gold coins); rouleau (a roll of coins in paper), *see also* MONEY.

COLOURS—a mass, rainbow, range *or* palette of colours; a phantasmagoria of bright colours.

COLTS—a rage *or* rake of colts, *see also* HORSES.

COLORATURAS (singers)—a quaver of coloraturas.

COLUMNS—a group of columns.

COMFORTS—a confluence of comforts.

COMIC STORIES—a posy of comic stories.

COMMISSIONERS—a sitting of commissioners.

COMMODITIES—a profusion *or* store of commodities, *see also* PROVISIONS.

COMMONPLACES—a cento of commonplaces.

COMMUNICATIONS—a system of communications.

COMMUNISTS—a cell of communists.

COMMUTERS—a dash of commuters.

COMPLAINTS—a cartload *or* pack of complaints.

COMPLIMENTS—a faggot *or* load of compliments.

COMRADES, *see* FRIENDS, ACQUAINTANCES.

CONDENSERS—a battery of condensers.

CONES—cone-in-cone (a collection of parallel cones)

CONFETTI—a salvo of confetti.

CONIES, *see* RABBITS.

CONJECTURES—a web *or* plump of conjectures.

CONSONANTS—a clutter of consonants.

CONSTABLES, *see* POLICE.

CONSPIRATORS—a combine of conspirators.

CONSTANCY—a dram of constancy (use negatively, i.e., somebody has not a dram of constancy)

CONTRADICTIONS—a concatenation of bungles and contradictions; a mass of contradictions.

CONTROVERSIES—a welter of controversies.

CONVICTS—a gang of convicts.

COOKS—a hastiness *or* a temperance of cooks; kitchenry (a group of servants engaged in the kitchen)

COOPERS—a gang of coopers.

COOTS—a covert; a flock *or* pod of coots.

COQUETTES—a consult of coquettes.

CORDS—a clew *or* raffle of cords.

CORMORANTS—a colony of cormorants; a flight of cormorants.

CORN *or* **WHEAT**—a congiary (a donation *or* largess); a crop, firlot, garb (a bundle); knitch; hill; hurry, sheaf *or* stack of corn *or* wheat.

CORVISERS (shoemakers)—a trinket of corvisers (15th century)

COUNCILLORS—a consult *or* consistory of councillors (advisers)

COURTESANS—a college of courtesans, *see also* PROSTITUTES.

COURTESY—an embroidery of courtesy.

COURTIERS—a fawning *or* threatening of courtiers; the court (courtiers, *collectively*); a train (courtiers, *collectively*)

COVENANTERS—a conventicle of covenanters.

COWARDS—a pack *or* farrago of cowardice.

COWS, *see* CATTLE.

COXCOMBS—a case *or* covey of coxcombs.

CRANES—a flock, herd, sedge, siege or sege of cranes.

CREDITORS—a curse of creditors.

CRICKETERS—an eleven, a field.

CRITICS—a crew of critics; a shrivel of critics.

CROCODILES—a nest *or* bask of crocodiles.

CROWS—a parcel, hover *or* murder of crows.

CRYSTALS—a crop *or* cluster of crystals.

CUBS—a litter of cubs.

CUCKOLDS—an incredibility of cuckolds (15th century)

CUNNING—a farrago of cunning.

CURATES, *see* CLERGY.

CURLEW—a herd of curlew.

CURLING PLAYERS—a core of curling players.

CURS (dogs)—a cowardice of curs (15th century)

CURVES (geometric)—a family of curves.

CUT-PURSES—a quest of cut-purses.

CUTLERY—a canteen of cutlery; plate (cutlery, *collectively*), *see also* DISHES.

CYCLISTS—a meet of cyclists; a wobble of cyclists.

DAFFODILS—a host of golden daffodils.

DAMES—a parcel of fair dames.

DANCERS—a choir, team *or* troupe of dancers; a morris (a team of morris dancers)

DAUBERS—a squat of daubers (15th century, a man who plastered with daub the daub-and-wattle walls of the cottages)

DAUGHTERS—a brood of daughters.

DAYS—a leash of days (three)

DEANS—a decanter of deans; a decorum of deans (in their stalls), *see also* CLERGY.

DEBATERS—a team *or* host of debaters.

DEBRIS—brash (debris, *collectively*)

DEBUTANTES—delirium of debutantes.

DECAY—a fry of foul decay.

DEER—a bevy of roe deer (six head); a brace of bucks; a game of red deer; a great bevy of roe deer (twelve deer); a great herd of deer (eighty head); a herd of deer; a leash of deer (three); a little herd of deer (twenty head); a middle bevy of roe deer (ten head); a middle herd of deer (forty head); quarry (a heap of dead deer, killed in the hunt); a rangale *or* common herd of deer.

DEFORMITIES—a miscellany of deformities.

DEITIES (Gods)—rabble of gods; a rabble of licentious deities; triad of deities (three); a tripletrine (the nine muses), *see also* GODS.

DELEGATES—a convention, delegation, deputation *or* legacy of delegates.

DENTISTS—a wince of dentists.

DERMATOLOGISTS—a rash of dermatologists.

DESPAIR—salvos of despair.

DESTROYERS (maritime)—a flotilla of destroyers.

DEVILS—an assembly, pandemonium *or* posse of devils; a phalanstery of all the fiends.

DIAGNOSTICIANS—a flutter of diagnosticians.

DIAMONDS—a parcel of diamonds.

DICE—a bale of dice (a set)

DIN (noise), *see* SOUNDS.

DINERS—a feast (diners, *collectively*); a sitting (diners, *collectively*)

DIPLOMATISTS—a legation (diplomatists, *collectively*)

DIRECTORS—a board of directors.

DISCUSSION—a crop of petty discussions; a sea of discussions.

DISHES—a garnish of dishes (set for the table); a pile, rabble *or* stack of dishes.

DIVINES (clergy)—a body of divinity, *see also* CLERGY.

DOCTORS—a council of physicians; a conventicle *or* race of doctors; a doctrine (doctors, *collectively*)

DOCTRINE—a covey of doctrines; a screed of doctrine.

DOCUMENTS—a calendar, chartulary *or* schedule of documents; an archive (a collection of documents)

DOGFISH—a troop of dogfish.

DOGS—a bench (show dogs), brace (two), gang, legion, kennel, pack *or* stud of dogs; a cowardice of curs; a doggery (dogs, *collectively*); a huddle *or* litter of puppies.

DOLPHINS—a team or school of dolphins.

DOMESTIC AFFECTIONS—a chaplet of domestic affections.

DOMINOES—a nieveful of dominoes (a handful)

DONS—a faculty (dons, *collectively*); an obscuration of dons.

DORMICE—a nest of dormice.

DOTTREL—a trip of dottrel.

DOUBTS—a farrago *or* rabble of doubts; a gale of doubt and apprehension.

DOVES—a duet, dule, dole *or* flight of doves; a pitying of turtle doves; a true love of turtle doves.

DOWAGERS—a frost of dowagers.

DRAPERIES—a raffle of flying draperies.

DRAWERS—a chest of drawers.

DREAMS—an embroidery of dreams.

DRINKS—a round of drinks; a bevy (a drinking company)

DRUGS—a druggery (drugs, *collectively*); a codex (a list of drugs)

DRUM-BEATS—a battery of drum-beats; a roll of drum-beats.

DRUNKS—a stone *or* a load of drunks.

DUCKS—a badelynge, brace (two), bunch, mob, paddling, plump, safe skein (in flight), sord, sore, team *or* waddling of ducks; a fleet of ducklings; brood of young ducks.

DUKES—a bundle of dukes.

DUNBIRDS—a rush *or* flight of dunbirds.

DUNLINS—a fling of dunlins.

DUST—a drift *or* cloud of dust.

DUTIES—a rota, round *or* schedule of duties.

DYNAMITE—a cake *or* stick of dynamite.

DYNAMOS—a battery of dynamos.

EAGLES—an aerie *or* brood of eagles; convocation of eagles.

EARTH—an accretion, balk *or* pocket of earth.

ECHOES—a choir of echoes.

ECONOMISTS—a recession of economists.

EDITORS—an erudition of editors.

EDUCATION—a college of students, a commonwealth of learning, *see also* KNOWLEDGE.

EELS—a bed, bind (10 sticks, i.e., 250 eels), draft (20 lb.), fry *or* swarm of eels.

EGGS—a brood, clutch, laughter, nide (geese or pheasants eggs), set *or* sitting of eggs.

ELDERS—a presbytery (a body of elders of the church)

ELECTRIC LIGHTS—a bank *or* battery of lights.

ELEPHANTS—a flock, herd *or* parade of elephants.

ELKS—a gang of elks.

ELOQUENCE—floods *or* torrents of eloquence.

EMIGRANTS—a stream of emigrants.

EMOTIONS—a flock of affections; an outgush of emotion, range of emotions; tide of feeling; transports of delight; tribute of affection; tumult of passions and spirits; wave of emotion, *see also* FEELINGS, HATE, LAUGHTER, etc.

ENERGY—an accumulation *or* outburst of energy.

ENGAGEMENTS—a press of engagements.

ENTHUSIASTS—a posse of enthusiasts; a wave of enthusiasm; a fanclub (enthusiasts, *collectively*)

EPICS—a cycle of epics.

EPIGRAMS—an anthology of epigrams.

EQUESTRIANS—a prance of equestrians, *see also* HORSEMEN.

ERRORS—a hotchpotch *or* raff of errors; a rhapsody of errors and calumnies.

EVENTS—a chain, chapter *or* tide of events, *see also* CIRCUMSTANCES.

EVIDENCE—a scrap or a mass of evidence, also a chain of evidence (i.e., one piece leading to another)

EVIL—an accumulation *or* nest of evil.

EXAMINERS—a gloat of examiners.

EXAMPLES—a sea of examples.

EXCUSES—a string of excuses.

EXECUTIONERS—a college of executioners.

EXPERTS—a panel of experts.

EXPLOSIONS—a concatenation of explosions (one after another); a burst of explosions.

FABRIC—a bolt of fabric.

FACES—a parcel of wry faces; a sea of faces.

FACTORS—a factory (body of factors or workmen)

FACTS—an array, body, camp, hoard, host *or* succession of facts.

FAGGOTS (wood)—a bundle of faggots.

FAIRIES—a bevy of fairies.

FALCONS—a cast of falcons (two)

FAMILY—a brood of daughters; a descent of relatives; a mess of sons; *also* folk, kin, generation (used *collectively*)

FANATICS—an academy of fanaticism; a rant of fanatics.

FANCY—an exuberance of fancy.

FAULTS—a mass of faults.

FAVOURS—a multitude of favours.

FEARS—a farrago of fears; a fusillade of terror.

FEATHERS—a bouquet, bush, peck, pencil, tuft of feathers; a phantasmagoria of coloured feathers and spangles.

FEELINGS—a tide *or* wealth of feeling, *see also* EMOTIONS.

FELICITY—a concatenation of felicity.

FELLOWS—a raff *or* crowd of fellows, fellowed (*collectively*)

FENCES—a flight of fences (horse-racing)

FERNS—a fernery (ferns, *collectively*)

FERRETS—a busyness; fesnyng *or* fesynes of ferrets.

FESTOONS—festoonery (festoons, *collectively*)

FIBRES—a fascicle *or* flake of fibres.

FIDDLERS—a consort *or* covey of fiddlers (violinists)

FIGS—a sort of figs.

FIGURES—an array *or* column of figures (i.e., numbers); a phantasmagoria of figures (persons)

FINCHES—a chirm of finches (from the meaning a din or chatter), *also* a charm of finches.

FIRE—a ball *or* column of fire.

FIREWORKS—a bouquet (a large flight of rockets), a cascade, display *or* fare of fireworks.

FISH—a catch, cran, draught, drave (a haul or shoal), a flote, flutter (of jellyfish), haul (single draught), school, flock; leash (three) *or* run of fish; shoal, shot (single draught) *or* skull (shoal) of fish.

FISHERMEN—a drift, colony, exaggeration of fishermen, a fishery (fishermen, *collectively*)

FISH-HOOKS—a flight of fish-hooks (used in a spinning trace)

FISHING NETS—a drift *or* shot of fishing nets.

FISTS—a bunch of fives.

FIVE—pented (five years); quinary (set of five things); quintette (five people); quintuplet (five children born in the same labour)

FLAMES—a jet *or* sheaf of flame; a pyramid of flames.

FLAMINGOES—a stand of flamingoes.

FLATS—a block of flats.

FLATTERERS—a fare of flatterers, fools and cheaters.

FLAX—a beat, head (bundle), lock, shive, stook *or* strike of flax.

FLIES—business, cloud, community, fare, rabble *or* swarm of flies; a grist of flies.

FLOWERS—an anthology, boughpot, bouquet, bunch, chaplet, conglomerate, embroidery, fascicle, festoon, garland, nosegay, poesy, posy, pot-pourri (of flower perfumes), sheaf, spray, tress of flowers; a florilegium or flowerage (flowers, *collectively*); wreath.

FLYING-DRAPERIES—a raffle of flying draperies.

FOLIAGE—a bush (foliage, *collectively*); an exuberance of foliage, *see also* BRANCH, BUSHES.

FOLLIES—a bundle of follies; a broad *or* mass of folly, *see also* FOOLS.

FOLK—a raft *or* shock of folk, *see also* FAMILY.

FOLLOWERS—a band or power of followers; a following (followers, *collectively*), *see also* FRIENDS.

FOOD—a collation (a meal usually cold); oodles of food (a large amount); a pittance of food (a small amount); a mess of peas, beans; a potage, provisions, a spread (all food, *collectively*)

FOOLS—a fare of flatterers, fools and cheaters; a nest *or* pack of fools; a fooliaminy (fools, *collectively*)

FOOTBALLERS—an eleven *or* a team (footballers, *collectively*); a gate of spectators or of supporters.

FORCES AND PASSIONS—a sea of forces and passions.

FORESTERS—a stalk of foresters.

FORESTS—a girdle of forests; a mantle of forests.

FORTS—a ring of forts.

FORTUNE—an accumulation of fortune.

FOUR—quarternary *or* quarternion (four things or a group of four facts *or* circumstances); quartet (four people); quadrille; quads (four children born in the same labour)

FOWLS—a roost of fowls; a scry of fowls, *see also* CHICKEN, HENS.

FOXES—a brace (two dens of fox families); an earth, leash (three) *or* skulk of foxes.

FOXHUNTERS—the hunt (foxhunters, *collectively*)

FRAGMENTS—a brash, conglomerate, shive *or* shave of fragments.

FRAGRANCE—a gale of fragrance.

FREEMASONS, *see* MASONS.

FRIARS—a chapter, convents, fratry, friary (friars, *collectively*); a skulk of friars, *see also* CLERGY, MONKS.

FRIENDS—a circle of acquaintances *or* friends; clique; a cohort of acquaintances; a comitatus; a comradery; a flock of friends.

FROGS—a colony of frogs; a froggery (frogs, *collectively*); an army of frogs.

FRONDS—frondage (fronds, *collectively*)

FRUIT—fruitage, fruitery, yield (all taken *collectively*)

FUGITIVES—a band of fugitives.

FUNERALS—an unction of undertakers; a cortège, a funeral train.

FURNITURE SHOPS—congeries of furniture shops.

FURS—a mantle (a quantity of furs)

GAMBLERS—talent (gamblers, *collectively*)

GAME—a bag of game.

GAMES—a set of games (as in tennis)

GARLANDS—garlandry (*collectively*); a rosary of garlands.

GEESE—a clutch, flock, gaggle, line, nide *or* skein (in flight), of geese, also a goosery (geese, *collectively*)

GELDINGS—a brace of geldings (two)

GENERALS—generality (generals, *collectively*)

GENIUS—a constellation of genius.

GENTLEMEN—a rout of gentlemen.

GEOLOGISTS—a conglomerate of geologists.

GHOSTS—a phantomtry *or* phantasmagoria (ghosts, *collectively*)

GIFTS—a shower of gifts.

GIN—a dram of gin.

GIPSIES—a crew of gipsies.

GIRAFFES—a herd *or* tower of giraffes.

GIRLS—a carol of virgins; a college of handmaidens; a covey; a crocodile (long line of girls, usually schoolgirls); a giggle of girls; a girlhood *or* girlery (girls, *collectively*), a parcel of girls; talent (girls, *collectively*), *see also* LADIES, VIRGINS, WOMEN.

GLADIATORS—a family.

GLASS—a bolt of molten glass; a crate *or* seam of glass.

GLORY—a sea of glory.

GNATS—a cloud, plague, rabble *or* swarm of gnats; horde of gnats.

GOATS—a flock, herd, tribe, trip *or* trippe of goats.

GOBLETS—a nest of goblets.

GODS—cabiri (the gods of Samothrace); a junta or pantheon of gods, *see also* DEITIES.

GOLD—pocket of nuggets.

GOLDFINCHES—a charm *or* chirm of goldfinches.

GOLD-LEAF—a book of gold-leaf.

GOODS *or* **GOOD**—abundance of good things; army of good words; congregation of goods; dram of well doing; fond of goods (a store); power of good; rosary of good works.

GOOSEPIMPLES—a crop of goosepimples.

GORILLAS—band of gorillas (usually male, with one or two females and young)

GOSHAWKS—a cast (two) *or* a flight of goshawks.

GOSSIPS—a gaggle of gossips; a gossiping *or* gossipry (gossips, *collectively*)

GOVERNESSES—a galaxy of governesses.

GRACE—an assemblage, a hoard *or* pittance of grace.

GRADUATES—an unemployment of graduates; gown.

GRAIN—a boll (6 bushels; also 140 lb.); a cast (an amount harvested); a cob (small stack); a garb (glean); gavel; glean; grist (amount brought to the mill at one time);

last reap (handful of grain); rick; seam (8 bushels); sheaf, stack; stoop of grain; a stook *or* shock of sheaves of corn, *see also* CORN.

GRAPES—bunch, cluster *or* raisin of grapes.

GRASS—math (an amount of mown grass); a tuft, tussock *or* whisk of grass; mop (tuft of grass)

GRASSHOPPERS—a cloud of grasshoppers.

GRAVEL—a bar of gravel.

GREYHOUNDS—a brace (two), leash *or* lece (three) of greyhounds.

GREYS (badgers) a cete of greys.

GRIEVANCES—a cartload, hoard *or* volley of grievances.

GROUSE—a brood, covey (single broods), harvest, jug (roosting), lak *or* lek (blackgrouse) *or* pack (several broods) of grouse.

GUARD—a watch (guards, *collectively*)

GUARDIANS—a board of guardians.

GUESTS—a feast (a company, *collectively*); a levee of guests.

GUILT—a load of guilt; a brood of guilty wives.

GULLS—a school of gulls; a colony *or* screech of gulls.

GUNPOWDER—a charge or keg of gunpowder.

GUNS *and* **GUNFIRE**—a battery of guns; a brace of pistols (two); a charge of gunpowder shot; a peal of artillery; a pile of arms and weapons; cannonry (cannons, *collectively*); gunnery (guns, *collectively*); platoon of gunfire (shots fired simultaneously); rafale (burst of several rounds of artillery); salvo of gunfire; stand of guns (game shooting); volley of gunfire.

GYNAECOLOGISTS—a smear of gynaecologists.

HAIL—a fall of hail.

HAIR—a cob of hair (a small bunch); a lock, pencil (small tuft of hair); tress, braid, plait, shock, tuft, tussock *or* whisk of hair; a palisade of stiff hairs (an unshaven chin)

HAIRDRESSERS—a swish of hairdressers.

HANDMAIDENS—a college of handmaidens.

HARES—a brace (two); down, flick, huske, kindle (of leverets), lease *or* leash (three), tripp of hares; a drove *or* trace of hares; a warren.

HARLOTS—a herd, *see also* PROSTITUTES.

HARPISTS—a melody of harpers (15th century)

HARTS—a herd of harts, *see also* DEER.

HATE—a harvest of hate.

HAWKS—an aerie, brood, cast (two), lece *or* leash (three), of hawks; a mews (collection of hawks moulting); a flight of goshawks.

HAWTHORN—quick (hawthorn, *collectively*)

HAY—a cob (small bunch), a cock; bottle, gavel, hurry (small load), knitch, lock, mow, tress, truss, wad, wisp of hay.

HAYWARDS—a waywardness of haywards (15th century)

HEADS—a sea of heads.

HEAT—a beam of heat.

HEATHEN—a covin of heathen; heathenry (the heathen, *collectively*)

HEDGE CLIPPINGS—a brash *or* quick of hedge clippings.

HEDGEHOGS—a nest of hedgehogs.

HEIRS—heritage, succession (heirs, *collectively*)

HELL—a posse of hell, *see also* DEVILS.

HEMP—a beat, glean *or* sheaf of hemp; a break of hemp.

HENS—a battery of boilers *or* hens; a brood, parcel *or* roost of hens; a mews (when hens are couped up for fattening); a concatenation of hens, *see also* CHICKEN, EGGS.

HERALDS—a college of heralds.

HERBS—bouquet, faggot, nosegay of herbs; herbarium, herbary.

HERDSMEN—a booly (company of herdsmen wandering with their cattle); a waywardness of haywards.

HERESIES *and* **HERETICS**—bundle *or* gang of heretics, conciliable (secret assembly of heretics); drove, mass *or* pack of heresies; rhapsody of condemned heresies.

HERMITS—an observance of hermits.

HERONS—a rookery (colony of herons); a sedge, sege, serge *or* siege of herons; on passage (in flight)

HERRING—cast (number thrown into vessel at one time); an army or glean of herring; a cade (720 herrings); a cran; last (12 barrels); school, shoal *or* warp (four) of herrings.

HIDES, *see* SKINS.

HIEROGLYPHS—a signary of hieroglyphs.

HIPPIES—a trip of hippies.

HIPPOPOTAMI—a school *or* bloat of hippopotami.

HOGS, *see* PIGS, BOARS, SWINE.

HOMILIES—postil of homilies.

HONOURS—accumulation *or* roster of honours.

HOPES—a farrago of hopes.

HOPS—pocket of hops (168 lb.)

HORNETS—bike or swarm of hornets.

HORSE SHOES—a gang (*or* set) of horse shoes.

HORSEMEN—a body of horse; cavalcade, cavalry, cornet of horse, a hunt, a prance of equestrians.

HORSES—a field (hunting horses); haras (wild horses or breeding mares); mews; a mob (Australian); a parcel, rag (colts); rake (colts); ruck (large number) of horses; a slate (a list of horses in a race); string of horses (racehorses); stud (mares); team (carriage or polo horses); a herd of horses.

HOTELIERS—a host of hoteliers, *see also* INNKEEPERS.

HOUNDS—cowardice of curs; a harl (three hounds); a meute, mute *or* pack of hounds; a kennel (hounds *or* dogs, *collectively*); a brace; a sute of bloodhounds; a cry of hounds; a kennel of rashes; a couple of running hounds; a stable; a leash (three)

HOUSEKEEPERS—a foresight of housekeepers.

HOUSES—a clump, cluster *or* terrace of houses; a troop of tenements.

HUMAN BEINGS, *see* PEOPLE.

HUMMOCKS—a nest of hummocks.

HUMOUR—a breed of wit, an embroidery of humour, a posy of comic stories, *see also* LAUGHTER.

HUMOURS—a miscellany of humours, *see also* EMOTIONS.

HUNTSMEN—a blast of hunters; a range of hunters (horses); a meet.

HURDLES—a flight of hurdles.

HUSBANDS—a multiplying of husbands; an unhappiness of husbands.

HUTS—hutting (huts, *collectively*); a rancho (huts, *collectively*)

HYMNS—an anthology of hymns.

HYPOCRITES—a congregation of hypocrites; a regiment of hypocrites.

IBEX—a herd of ibex.

IBISES—a colony of ibises.

ICE—a belt, brash (fragments), cake, drift, floe, pack, stream of ice; a patch of floating ice floes.

ICEBERGS—a cluster, pack *or* palisade (row) of icebergs.

IDEAS—an assemblage, chain, concatenation, heap, hotch-potch, huddle, parcel *or* profusion of ideas.

IDIOMS—a knot of idioms.

IMAGES—a host of images.

IMMORALITY—a drove of immoralities.

IMPERIAL GUARD—a school *or* troop of the Imperial Guard.

IMPERTINENCE—a rhapsody of impertinence.

IMPROBABILITIES—a faggot of improbabilities.

INCENSE—a cloud of incense.

INCIDENTS—a combination of incidents.

INFANTRY, *see* TROOPS.

INFANTS—a creche (infants, *collectively*)

INFIDELS—a plague of infidels, *see also* HEATHEN.

INFORMATION—a cloud, mine *or* wealth of information.

INIQUITY—a sink *or* pandemonium of iniquity.

INN-KEEPERS—a closing of taverners; a host of hoteliers; a landlordry (landlords, *collectively*); a laughter of ostlers; a promise of tapsters; also a cajolery of taverners.

INSECTS—a horde, nest, rabble *or* swarm of insects.

INSTRUMENTS—a case *or* concert of instruments.

INTRIGUERS—a cabal (intriguers as a group)

INVENTIONS—a budget of inventions.

IRE—accumulation of ire, *see also* ANGER, WRATH.

IRONMONGERS—a craft (ironmongers, *collectively*)

ISLANDS—an archipelago; a chain, cluster, crowd, group, fry, heap, knot, lac, lodge, network *or* pile of islands.

IVY—a bush of ivy (branches hung up as a vintner's sign)· a festoon of ivy.

JAYS—a party of jays; a band of jays.

JELLYFISH—a fluther *or* smack of jellyfish; a stuck *or* smuth of jellyfish.

JESUITS—a consult of Jesuits.

JEWELS—a cache, cascade, casket, *or* locket (a group of set jewels) of jewels; a ring of jewellers.

JEWS—a pack of jews; Jewry (jews, *collectively*), *see also* RABBIS.

JOBS—Jobbery (jobs, *collectively*)

JOURNALISTS—a chapel of journalists; the press; a raft of reporters, *see also* EDITORS.

JOYS—a confluence or exuberance of joys.

JUDGES—a bank *or* bench of judges; a court (all persons assembled to administer law); judicature *or* judiciary (judges, *collectively*); a mess of judges and barristers; a panel or quorum of judges; a sentence of judges; session (a group of judges in session), *see also* BARRISTERS, ATTORNEYS, LAW, LAWYERS.

JUGGLERS—a neverthriving of jugglers (15th century)

JURORS—a jury (the jurors, *collectively*); a damning of jurors; panel of jurors.

KANGAROOS—a mob *or* troop of kangaroos.

KEYS—a bunch of keys.

KINE (cattle)—a drove of kine.

KINGS—a leash of kings (three)

KITCHEN UTENSILS—a battery of kitchen utensils.

KITTENS—a kendle, kindle, kyndyll *or* nest of kittens; a brood *or* litter of kittens.

KNAVES—a pack, rayfull *or* raffle of knaves, a bachelry (knaves, *collectively*)

KNIGHTS—a banner, chapter, comitatus of knights; knightage; knighthood (knights, *collectively*); a rout of knights; a templar of Knights Templar.

KNOWLEDGE—an accumulation, round, smack, store of knowledge; a breed of thinkers; a chaos of accidental knowledge; a commonwealth of learning; a conglomerate of useful (or useless) knowledge; a constellation of genius; a dram, pittance, scrap or scattering of knowledge; a heap of learned men, a host of thoughts; resort of learned men; wealth of knowledge, *and* doctrine (doctors, i e., Ph.D.s, *collectively*)

LACE—a cascade *or* purl of lace.

LACKEYS—a cast of lackeys, *see also* SERVANTS.

LADIES—a bevy *or* range of ladies; ladyhood (ladies, *collectively*)

LAKES—a chain of lakes.

LAMBS—a cast *or* fall of lambs, *see also* SHEEP.

LAND—a parcel of land.

LANDLORDS—landlordry (landlords, *collectively*)

LANGUAGES—a babel of languages; a family of languages.

LAPWING—a deceit *or* desert of lapwing.

LARKS—a bevy, exaltation *or* flight of larks.

LAUGHTER—a chorus, gale, gust, peal, riot *or* wave of laughter *or* merriment; revelrout (a lively party of merrymakers)

LAVA—a flood of lava, a cascade of volcanic ash.

LAW—a body, canon, code, digest *or* library of law, *see also* BARRISTERS, JUDGES, LAWYERS.

LAWYERS—the bar (barristers and lawyers, *collectively*); a boredom of briefs; an eloquence, escheat *or* faculty of lawyers; gown (lawyers, *collectively*); a phalanx or sight of lawyers; a subtlety of sergeants, *see also* BARRISTERS, JUDGES, LAW.

LAYMEN—the laity, (laymen, *collectively*)

LEARNING, *see* KNOWLEDGE.

LEAVES—a levesel *or* sheaf of leaves; leafage *or* frondage (leaves *or* branches, *collectively*)

LEAVES (of a book)—a fascicle.

LEGATES—a legacy (Papal Legates)

LEGENDS—legendry (legends, *collectively*); a family of legends.

LENSES (light)—a battery of lenses.

LEOPARDS—a lepe *or* leap of leopards.

LEPERS—a colony of lepers.

LETTERS—a batch, file, shoal, stack *or* sheaf of letters, *also* a combination of letters (initial letters)

LEVERETS—a kindle of leverets.

LEYDEN JARS—a battery of Leyden jars.

LIBRARIANS—a sheaf *or* catalogue of librarians.

LIBRARIES—a consortium of university libraries.

LICE—a flock of lice.

LICENTIOUS DEITIES—a rabble of licentious deities.

LIES—a brood, cartload, crop, embroidery, farrago, pack, parcel, peck, string, tissue *or* web of lies.

LIGHT—a bank of electric lights; a battery of light, *also* of searchlights; a beam of light-rays and of sunlight; body of light; a brush of light rays; a burst of light; a cone *or* pencil of light-rays; a flood *or* ray of light; a sheaf of light-rays.

LINEN—a bunch of linen yarn (60 hanks); a bundle of linen yarn (20 hanks)

LINES—a network of lines; a sheaf of lines (geometry)

LINNETS—a parcel of linnets.

LIONS—a flock, pride or sowse of lions (sowse is used in the Egerton MSS.); a sawt *or* troop of lions.

LISTENERS—an auditory (a group of listeners); a circle of listeners.

LITERATURE—a casket of literary selections; a chrestomathy of literary passages; a collectanea; a confection of literature; a corpus (of writings on a subject); a literary circle; a miscellanea *or* miscellany; a posse of articles.

LOCAL GOVERNMENT AUTHORITIES—a consortia of local government authorities.

LOCKS (canal)—a flight of locks.

LOCUST—a cloud, plague *or* swarm of locust.

LOGS—a drive, pile *or* raft of logs.

LORRIES—a fleet of lorries.

LOVERS—a trance of lovers.

MACHINES—a battery of machines.

MACKEREL—a mess, pad (a measure of 60 mackerel) *or* shoal of mackerel.

MAGISTRATES—a bench *or* court (magistrates, *collectively*), *see also* LAWYERS.

MAGPIES—a tiding *or* tittering of magpies.

MAIDENS—a carol *or* a rage of maidens; college of handmaidens, *see also* GIRLS.

MAIDS OF HEAVEN (angels)—a bevy of maids of heaven.

MALEVOLENCE—a screed of malevolence.

MALLARD—a flush, lute, puddling, sord *or* sute of mallards.

MANNERS—a code of manners.

MANURE—a pie of manure.

MANUSCRIPTS, *see* DOCUMENTS.

MARES—a stud of mares; a haras of mares, *see also* HORSES.

MARINES—a mess (marines, *collectively*)

MARTINS—a richesse *or* richness of martins.

MARTYRS—an army *or* consistory of martyrs.

MASONS—a brotherhood (masons, *collectively*); a lodge of masons; the Craft (masons, *collectively*)

MASSEURS—a pummel of masseurs.

MASTERS—an example of masters (15th century)

MATADORS—a pavanne of matadors.

MATERIALS (textiles)—a bolt of cloth (40 yards); a bolt of silk (40 yards) a bolt of canvas (40 yards); a bunch of linen (60 hanks); a bundle of linen (20 hanks); a pad *or* skein of wool.

MATHEMATICS—a covey *or* parcel of mathematicians; a canon of mathematical tables.

MAXIMS—a gnomology of maxims.

MEAL—a grist (a supply of meal)

MELODIES—a quodlibet of melodies.

MEMORIES—a round of memories.

MEN—a covert, cordon, detachment, detail, host, pare *or* plump of men; a covin of wicked men; a fraternity *or* manhood (men, *collectively*), *see also* BACHELORS.

MERCHANTS—a caravan, convent *or* faith of merchants; merchantry (merchant, *collectively*)

MERCY—an abundance *or* well of mercy; a dram of mercy (used negatively)

MERLIN—a leash (three) of merlin.

MERRIMENT, *see* LAUGHTER.

MESSENGERS—a diligence of messengers (15th century)

METAPHORS—a mob of metaphors.

METEOROLOGISTS—a shower of meteorologists.

METEORS—a fall *or* swarm of meteors.

METHODISTS—a denomination (the members of the Methodist Church, *collectively*)

MICE—a colony, harvest *or* nest of mice.

MIDGES—a bite of midges.

MILES—a score of miles.

MILK—a mess of milk.

MILLINERS—a fraunch of milliners (15th century—fraunch means to eat ravenously, and is probably a pun)

MINERALS—a suite of minerals.

MINERS—a convocation of tinners; a core of miners, *also* a shift of miners.

MINES—a bal of mines (Cornish)

MINISTERS—a junto of ministers.

MINNOWS—a shoal of minnows.

MINSTRELS—a troupe of minstrels; a minstrelsy (minstrels, *collectively*)

MIRACLES—conjugation, field *or* nest of miracles.

MISERS—a horde of misers.

MISFORTUNES—an army *or* tissue of misfortunes.

MISTAKES—a mass of mistakes.

MITES—a mite of mites.

MODELS—a slouch of models.

MOLES—a company *or* labour of moles; a citadel of mole burrows.

MONASTERIES—a congregation (e.g., the Congregation of Cluny)

MONEY—a bundle of notes; a collation, fond (a store), lock, mint, oodles (a lot), parcel, pile, pot, power, sight, stock *or* wad of money; a flood of banknotes; a journey *or* rouleau of coins; a levy (or tax) of money, pittance (a small amount), *see also* WEALTH.

MONKEYS—cartloads or troop of monkeys.

MONKS—an abomination of monks; a canon of monastic rule; a cell (small religious group or community connected to a monastery or convent); cenoby of monks; a congregation of monasteries; a convent, monkery *or* monkhood, monkship (monks, *collectively*); an observance of monks, *see also* FRIARS, CLERGY, MONASTERIES.

MOORHENS—a plump of moorhens.

MOOSE—a herd of moose.

MORALITY—a cycle of morality.

MORRIS DANCERS—a morris (morris dancers, *collectively*)

MOSQUITOES—a scourge of mosquitoes.

MOTHERS—a consternation of mothers.

MOTOR CARS—a fleet of cars; a motorcade (a procession of cars)

MOUNTAINS—a chain, knot (where the chains meet), palisade (a row), rain *or* range of mountains.

MOURNERS—a convoy *or* cortège of mourners.

MUDHENS—a fleet of mudhens.

MULES—a baren, barren, mulada, rake *or* span of mules.

MURDERERS—a rabble of murderers.

MUSES—a choir of muses, the tripletrine (the nine muses)

MUSHROOMS—a ring of mushrooms.

MUSIC—a casket of musical selections; a cento (or patchwork) of music; a cavalcade of songs; a confection of music; congeries of ballads; a cycle of songs; a garland of songs; a medley, montage *or* olio of musical pieces; opus (collection of musical compositions); a school of music, a quod libet.

MUSICAL INSTRUMENTS—a concert (*or* set) of instruments.

MUSICIANS—a band; a concert; a company of musicians; a consort (of viols or fiddlers); a melody of harpers; a group; a minstrelsy; an orchestra; a pluck of shawmers (a medieval instrument of the oboe type)

MUSKETS—musketry (muskets, *collectively*)

MUSLIN—a piece of muslin (12 yards)

MUSSELS—a bed of mussels.

MYTHS—a family of myths.

NABOBS—nabobery (nabobs, *collectively*)

NAMES—onomastican; a crowd of names.

NASTINESS—a cataract of nastiness.

NATIONS—a confederacy, a league *or* rhapsody of nations.

NETS—shot (the entire number of fishing nets thrown at one time)

NEWS—a budget *or* scrap of news.

NEWSPAPERS—a file of newspapers, the press (newspapers, reporters and staff, *collectively*)

NIGHT CAPS—a nest of night caps.

NIGHTINGALES—a watch of nightingales.

NIGHTWATCHMEN—a pallor of nightwatchmen.

NOISES, *see* SOUNDS.

NONSENSE—a pack, rhapsody *or* rigmarole of nonsense.

NOTES—a batch *or* screed of notes (i.e., writings); a bundle of notes (i.e., money)

NUGGETS (gold, etc.)—a pocket of nuggets.

NUNS—a convent *or* nunnery (nuns, *collectively*); a flap *or* superfluity (15th century) of nuns.

NUTS—a cluster *or* set of nuts.

OARS—a gang of oars.

OATHS—a chorus of bad language; fusillades of swearing; round of abuse; salvo of oaths; streams of abuse; a string of oaths; torrents *or* a volley of oaths.

OATS—a garb of oats.

OBSERVATIONS—a parcel of observations.

ODDFELLOWS—a Temple (Oddfellows, *collectively*)

ODDS AND ENDS—a host of odds and ends.

OFFICERS—an execution (15th century), mess or slate (a list) of officers.

OFFICIALS—a bench (officials, *collectively*)

OIL—a river of oil.

OLD GUARD—a slumber of old guard.

OLD MEN—a gerontocracy (government by old men)

ONIONS—a rope *or* string of onions.

ONLOOKERS—a circle of onlookers.

OPINIONS—a body, consensus, library, lurry, weight *or* welter of opinions.

OPPORTUNITY—a gale of opportunity.

ORCHIDS—a coterie of orchids.

ORE—a charge of ore (a quantity to fill furnace).

ORGANS—a bank *or* bench of organ keys; a rank of organ-pipes.

ORTHOPAEDISTS—a brace of orthopaedists.

OSIERS (willows used in basketry)—a bolt of osiers.

OSTEOPATHS—a joint of osteopaths.

OSTLERS, *see* INNKEEPERS.

OTTERS—a bevy or lodge of otters.

OUTBUILDINGS—a range of outbuildings.

OUTLAWS—a band *or* nest of outlaws.

OWLS—a parliament *or* stare of owls.

OXBIRDS—a fling of oxbirds.

OXEN—a drove, herd, meinie, team *or* yoke of oxen.

OYSTERS—a bed, cast, clam, fry (the young), hive, set (a crop) *or* warp (four) of oysters.

PAGODAS—a lac of pagodas.

PAIN—a plump of pain.

PAINT—a cake of paint.

PAINTERS—a curse, illusion, madder, misbelief *or* school of painters, *see also* ARTISTS.

PAINTINGS, *see* PICTURES.

PALM TREES—a knot of palm trees.

PAMPHLETS—a flock *or* school of pamphlets.

PANEGYRICS—cataracts of panegyrics.

PAPAL BULLS—a bullary (papal bulls, *collectively*)

PAPER AND PAPERS—a book of papers; bundle (two reams); dossier, file, litter (disorderly collection) *or* quire (24 sheets) of paper; a ream (flat sheets); a token (250 printed impressions); a pad (writing paper) of paper.

PAPISTS—a brigade of papists; a bulk of popery, *see also* CATHOLICS.

PARADOXES—a budget of paradoxes.

PARASITES—a consort *or* herd of parasites.

PARDONERS—a lying of pardoners.

PARENTS—a persistence of parents; parentage (parents, *collectively*)

PARLIAMENT—a House of Commons, Lords or Representatives, a sitting; *or* a lobby of M.P.s.

PARROTS—a company, flock, pandemonium of parrots; *also* a psittacosis.

PARTRIDGE—a bew, brace (two), clutch, covey, jug *or* leash (three), a warren of partridge.

PASSIONS—a bust of passion; a legion, rabble, sea *or* tumult of passions.

PATERNOSTERS—a belt of paternosters.

PATIENTS—a panel of patients.

PATRIARCHS—a bunch of patriarchs.

PATRIOTISM—a seeth of patriotic feelings.

PAUPERS—a poverty of paupers.

PEACE—a harvest of peace.

PEACOCKS—a muster, ostentation or pride of peacocks.

PEARLS—a network, rope *or* string of pearls.

PEASANTS—peasantry (peasants, *collectively*)

PEAS—a mess *or* pod of peas.

PEBBLES—a beach (pebbles, *collectively*)

PEDLARS—malpertness of pedlars.

PEERS—peerage (peers *collectively*)

PEKINGESE—a pomp of pekingese.

PELLETS—shot (pellets, *collectively*)

PENGUINS—a parcel *or* rookery of penguins.

PEOPLE—an assembly; audience; bike; chain; circle; clan; commonalty; concourse; confluence; confusion; congregation (religious); convention; convocation; crowd; crush; democracy (population of a democratic state);

demos (the population of a Greek state); denomication (society or sect of people with same interest—often religious); faction (a group at odds with others); fry *or* small fry (crowd of insignificant people); gallery; gang; host; knot (small group); lurry (confused group); mob; multitude; parcel; press; queue; raquet (group at a private house); raft; ring; score; sea of heads *or* faces; shoal; serry (crowded together); slew; stream; throng, *see also* PERSONS, FRIENDS.

PEPPER—a peck *or* a sprinkling of pepper.

PERCH—a pack *or* shoal of perch.

PERFECTION—a girdle of perfection.

PERFUMES—a gale (strong waft); pot-pourri (a mixture, often ill-chosen)

PERSONALITIES—a fusillade of personalities.

PERSONS—a clique (exclusive group). coterie (social group); claque of people, *see also* PEOPLE.

PEWS—pewing, pewage (pews, *collectively*)

PHANTOMS—phantomtry *or* phantasmagoria (phantoms, *collectively*)

PHEASANTS—a bouquet of pheasants (the flight of a flock from the beaters); a brace (two); a brood; an eye; a flock; a head (a large number); a nest, nide *or* nye of pheasants; a school *or* warren of pheasants.

PHILOSOPHERS AND PHILOSOPHIES—a school, sect *or* wrangle of philosophers; a system of philosophy.

PHRASES—a mint of phrases; a phraseology.

PHYSICIANS, *see* DOCTORS.

PHYSICISTS—a nucleus of physicists.

PIANISTS—a pounding of pianists.

PICKPOCKETS—a school of pickpockets.

PICTURES—canvas (paintings, *collectively*); an olio (a collection of miscellaneous paintings); a rabble; a sky of paintings (top row in a gallery)

PIGEONS—a flight, flock or loft of pigeons.

PIGS—a drove, a fare (litter), a flock of pigs; a hoggery (pigs, *collectively*); a litter (young); a sounder of pigs; a nest of trotters, *see also* BOARS, SWINE.

PIKE—a brace of pike.

PILCHARDS—a school *or* shoal of pilchards.

PILES—a spiling of piles.

PILGRIMS—a band, caravan *or* meinie of pilgrims.

PILLARS—an avenue, a group of pillars; a range *or* row of pillars; pillaring (pillars, *collectively*)

PIPERS—a verty of pipers; a skirl of pipers (musicians)

PIPES—a coil of pipes; compages of pipes and vessels; piping (pipes, *collectively*); a range *or* stack of pipes.

PIRATES—a horde, nest *or* crew of pirates.

PISTOLS—a brace (two) *or* case (two) of pistols.

PLANETS—a choir, chorus *or* conjuncture of planets.

PLANTS—a centeemer (large number); a clump, meinie *or* tuft of plants; a herbarium (dried flowers)

PLATE (cutlery)—a service *or* canteen of cutlery.

PLAYERS (actors)—company, troupe *or* band of players.

PLEASURES—a circle, party, pinch (small number) *or* round of pleasures.

PLOUGHS—a gang (a set of ploughs)

PLOVERS—a band, congregation, flight, leach, leash; stand *or* wing of plovers.

PLUMBERS—a flush of plumbers.

POCHARD (the male of the dunbird)—a rash, flight, knob of pochard; a diving of teal; a bunch of teal.

POEMS—an anthology of poems; a cento (patchwork) of verses; a cycle of poems or sonnets; a cento of verses; a divan; floriligium; macaroni (a medley of poetry); olio of verses (collection of miscellaneous verses); posy *or* rosary of poetry; a screed *or* treasury of poems.

POETS—a gang of poets; a pleiad (seven major poets of a period)

POISON—a dram of poison.

POKER PLAYERS—a stud (*collectively*)

POLICE—constabulary (*collectively*); a cordon *or* detachment, posse, clutch *or* patrol of police.

POLITICS AND POLITICIANS—a batch of politics; a cabal, caucus, cave *or* party of politicians (a cave is a small group who secede from the main party); a camarilla (a group of secret or irresponsible politicians); a coalition or junto (usually used for ministers); consistory of senators; disagreement of statesmen; The House (British M.P.s, *collectively*) *or* The Commons; a knot, legation *or* lobby of M.P.s; an odium *or* round of politicians.

POLO TEAM—a four.

PONIES—a herd or string of ponies, *see also* HORSES.

POOR PEOPLE—a poverty (*collectively*)

POPERY, *see* PAPISTS, CATHOLICS.

POPULATION—a congestion of population.

PORPOISES—a gam, herd, pod, school *or* turmoil of porpoises.

PORTERS—a safeguard of porters.

POSSIBILITIES—a chapter of possibilities.

POSTS—a forest *or* row of posts.

POTAGE—a mess of potage.

POTATOES—a camp (ridge-shaped heap), hill *or* pie of potatoes.

POULTRY—a run of poultry, *see also* CHICKEN, HENS.

POWER—accumulation of power.

PRAISE—a gale *or* paeon of praise; a sea of acclamation.

PRAYERS—a belt of paternosters; a century, chaplet, decade (ten) *or* rosary of prayers.

PREACHERS—a converting of preachers, *see also* CLERGY.

PRELATES—a conclave of prelates; a cone of prelacy (exclusive group); pontificate; prelacy; synod (prelates, *collectively*)

PRESENTS—a congiary (gifts given in Roman times); a shower of presents or gifts.

PRESUMPTIONS—a plump of presumptions.

PRIESTS—a convocation of clergy; clergy (*collectively*); a discretion, mass *or* scourge of priests; a phyle of priests (Greek)

PRINCES—a league *or* state of princes.

PRINCIPLES—a conjuncture of principles.

PRINTERS—a chapel of printers.

PRISONS AND PRISONERS—a battery of prisons; a gang *or* pity of prisoners.

PROCTOLOGISTS—a pile of proctologists.

PROFANITIES—a nest of profanities, *see also* OATHS.

PROMISES—a profusion of promises.

PROOF—a chain of proof.

PROPHETS—a bunch, company *or* flock of prophets.

PROSE—an anthology *or* miscellany of prose.

PROSTITUTES—a rookery (*collectively*); an anthology of pros; a consult of coquettes; a herd of harlots; a blast of strumpets; a jam of tarts, *see also* COURTESANS.

PROVERBS—a flotilla of proverbs.

PROVISIONS—a cache, hoard *or* store of provisions.

PRUNES—a nieveful of prunes.

PSYCHOANALYSTS—a complex of psychoanalysts.

PTARMIGANS—a covey of ptarmigans.

PUPILS—a class, dilation, range *or* school of pupils.

PUPPIES, *see* DOGS.

PYE, *see* MAGPIES.

QUAIL—a bevy, covey *or* jug of quail.

QUALITIES—a bundle of qualities; a congregation of fine qualities.

QUESTIONS—a host *or* multitude of questions; a questionnaire.

QUOTATIONS—a mellificium *or* rosary of quotations.

RABBIS—a rabbin *or* rabbinite.

RABBIT HUTCHES—a rabbitry (*collectively*)

RABBITS—bevy or bury of conies; colony, flick, kindle *or* nest of rabbits; a game of conies, a warren.

RACHES—a kennel of raches.

RAILLERY—a field of raillery.

RAILS—a flight of rails.

RAILWAYS—a network or system of railways.

RAIN—a brash (sudden dash of rain), a fall, a flurry, an oncome (heavy fall); a pash, a rash, a sheaf, a shower, a skelp (heavy fall), a sprinkling of rain.

RAISINS (fruit)—a frail (quantity varying from 32 lb. to 75 lb.); a sort of raisins.

RANTERS—a posse of ranters.

RAPIERS—a case (two) of rapiers.

RAVENS—an aerie *or* unkindness of ravens.

RAYS—a beam, a bundle, a pencil *or* sheaf of light rays.

READERS—an audience; a circle; a horde of young readers, a readership (*collectively*)

REAPERS—a reap (reapers, *collectively*)

REASONING—a chain, a pittance (small amount) *or* a sequence of reasoning.

REASONS—a library, a mint *or* a rabble of reasons.

REDWING—a crowd of redwing.

REEDS—a clump *or* knichet (handful) of reeds.

REFUSE—a fullage, litter, a midden *or* peltry of refuse.

REGICIDES—a horde of regicides.

RELATIVES—a descent of relatives, kindred.

RELIGIONS—an olio of various religions; an accrescence of belief, *see also* CLERGY.

REMEDIES—a rabble of remedies.

RENEGADES—a bevy of renegades.

REPORTERS, *see* JOURNALISTS.

REPROACHES—a legion of reproaches.

REPTILES—a bed of reptiles, *see also* SNAKES.

RESEARCH—avenues of research.

RETAINERS—a livery *or* ging (retainers, *collectively*), *see also* SERVANTS, BUTLERS, WAITERS.

REVELLERS—a revelrout (a lively crowd of party-goers)

REVOLUTIONS—a series of revolutions.

RHINOCEROS—a crash *or* stubbornness of rhinoceros.

RIBBONS—an echelle *or* a festoon of ribbons.

RIFLES—a stack of rifles (3 rifles stacked in a pyramid)

RIOTERS—a riotry (*collectively*)

RIVALS—a crowd of rivals.

RIVERS—a network of rivers.

ROACH—a shoal of roach.

ROBBERS—a band *or* nest of robbers; a brigandage *or* latriciny (*collectively*), *see also* BANDITS, BRIGANDS, THIEVES.

ROCKS—a cord (a measure) of rock; congeries of rock; a heap *or* pile of rocks.

ROCKETS—a bouquet, a cascade *or* a salvo of rockets.

ROES, *see* DEER.

ROMANS—a riot of Romans.

ROOKS—a building, a clamour, a colony of rooks; a rookery (rooks' nest, *collectively*)

ROOMS—a suite of rooms.

ROOTS—a fascicle *or* knot of roots.

ROPES—a network of ropes.

ROSES—a bouquet *or* bunch, a rosary *or* spray of roses; a bed (bushes)

ROWING—an eight; a four; a pair.

RUFFIANS—a gang of ruffians; brigandage (*collectively*)

RUFFS—a hill of ruffs.

RUGBY—a fifteen (the players, *collectively*)

RULES—a code of rules; a pie (collection of rules)

RUMOURS—a nest of rumours.

RUNNERS (athletics)—a field (*collectively*)

RUPEES—a lac (a large number, specifically 100,000)

RUSHES—a faggot *or* gavel of rushes.

RYE—a sheaf of rye; shock of sheaves.

SAILORS—a crew *or* draft (*collectively*); the kippage (a ship's crew); the navy (*collectively*)

SAILS—a cloud, a crowd, a press of sails; a gang of shrouds; canvas *or* outfit (sails, *collectively*); sailrife, *see also* SHIPS.

SAINTS—a calendar, canon, a communion *or* consistory of saints.

SALAD—a collation.

SALESMEN—a sample of salesmen; a haggle of vendors.

SALMON—a bind (fourteen gallons) *or* run of salmon.

SALT—a pinch of salt.

SAND—a balk, a bank, a beach, a bor, a drift, a mass, a pillar, a seam *or* wreath of sand.

SANDPIPERS—a fling of sandpipers.

SAUSAGES—a string of sausages.

SAVAGES—a horde *or* tribe of savages; a savagery *or* savagedom (*collectively*)

SAWS—a gang of saws (a set)

SCAFFOLDING POLES—a forest of scaffolding poles.

SCHOLARS, *see* ACADEMICS, PUPILS.

SCHOOLBOYS—a pack *or* rabble of schoolboys.

SCORPIONS—a bed *or* nest of scorpions.

SCOTS—a disworship of Scots (15th century)

SCRIPTURE—a body, a cento *or* code of scripture.

SEABIRDS—raft (at sea); rookery (a large colony); a sedge, sege *or* siege.

SEAFOWL—a cloud of seafowl.

SEALS—a flock, a herd, a plump, a pod *or* a rookery of seals.

SEAMSTRESSES—a scolding of kempsters (15th century)

SEARCHLIGHT—a battery of searchlights.

SEASONS—a cycle of seasons.

SEAWEED—kelp.

SECRETS—a hoard of secrets.

SEED—a cast (amount scattered at one time)

SELECTIONS—a faggot of selections.

SENATORS—a consistory *or* senate of senators.

SENSATIONS—a bundle of sensations.

SENTIMENTS—a train of happy sentiments, *see also* EMOTIONS, FEELINGS.

SEPARATISTS—a knot of separatists.

SERGEANTS—a subtlety of sergeants (lawyers)

SERVANTS—a heap, obeisance of servants; a kitchenry, retinue, servantry *or* staff (servants, *collectively*), *see also* BUTLERS, RETAINERS, WAITERS.

SEWERS—a credence of sewers (servants in charge of serving the dishes or serving water for washing the hands of the guests)

SHARES—a block of bonds or shares.

SHAWMERS—a pluck of shawmers (players of the medieval instrument called the shawm, similar to an oboe)

SHEAVES OF GRAIN—a shock *or* stook of sheaves.

SHEEP—a bought (ewes at milking time); a cast of lambs; a drift, a drove, a flock, a fold, a hurtle, a meinie, a parcel or a trip of sheep; a fall of lambs; a mob of sheep (Australian); a cast of lambs; a down of sheep.

SHELDRAKE—a dopping of sheldrake.

SHELVES—a nest of shelves; shelving (*collectively*)

SHERIFFS—a posse of sheriffs.

SHIPS—an armada of ships; a boatery (*collectively*); a bridge of boats; a brood of small boats; a bulk of ships (a large mass); a caravan or fleet of merchant ships; a company (merchant ships); a consort *or* convoy of ships; craft (*collectively*); an echelon of vessels (in parallel lines); a fellowship of vessels; a fleet; a flote; a flotilla of destroyers; a navy; a plump of yachts; sailrife *or* shipping (*collectively*); a squadron of ships; a succour of galleys.

SHOEMAKERS—a blackening of shoemakers, *see also* COBBLERS, SOUTERS.

SHOPKEEPERS—a haggle of vendors.

SHOPS—a chain of shops.

SHOT—a charge, a hail *or* a pile of shot, *see also* BULLETS.

SHOTS—a fusillade of shots.

SHOWDOGS—a bench of showdogs.

SHROUDS (sails)—a gang (a set of sails)

SHRUBS—a bosk, a shrubbery *or* bush (*collectively*); a palisade of shrubs.

SIGNALS—a code of signals; signary (signs, *collectively*)

SILK—a bolt (40 yards); a book (a bundle of skeins); a fangot of silk; a head (a bundle); a skein of silk.

SINGERS—a carol (a band of singers); a chapel, choir, a chorus of singers; a group; a quaver of coloraturas.

SINS—an army, bonds, a burden, a catalogue, a crowd, a fardel, a heap, a multitude of sins, *see also* CALUMNIES, IMMORALITY, INIQUITY.

SKATERS—an assemblage of skaters.

SKINS—a kip (a bundle of skins of small or young animals); a mantle of skins; a peltry; a timber of skins (40 skins of martins, ermines, sables or 120 other skins)

SLAVES—a bevy *or* gang of slaves; a helotry (*collectively*)

SLEET—a fall *or* shower of sleet.

SLUMBER—chains of slumber.

SMELTS (fish)—quantity of smelts.

SMOKE—a cloud, a column, a drift, a puff *or* a pillar of smoke, wreath.

SNAILS—an escargatoire; a rout *or* walk of snails.

SNAKES—a bed, a den of snakes, a knot of young snakes.

SNIPE—a couple (two dead); a leash (three dead); a walk, a whisp *or* a wisp of snipe.

SNOW—an accumulation of snow; a bank, a drift, a fall, a flurry *or* a girdle of snow; an oncome (heavy fall); a pash, rick *or* shower of snow, wreath.

SNUFF—a pinch of snuff.

SOAP—a bar or cake of soap.

SOBS—an outburst *or* storm of sobs or tears, *see also* TEARS.

SOLDIERS, *see* TROOPS.

SOMPNERS—an untruth of sompners (15th century—one who summons or calls people together)

SONGS, *see* MUSIC.

SONNETS, *see* POEMS.

SONS—a mess of sons (four)

SORROWS—a burden, fardel or pack of sorrows.

SOUNDS—babble of sounds; charivari of discordant noises; concert of terrific vociferation; congestion of tumult; conglomeration of sounds; girdle of din *or* noise; a medley of sounds; a pot-pourri of sounds.

SOUP—a slash of soup.

SOUTERS *or* **SOWTERS**—a bleche of souters.

SPANGLES—a phantasmagoria of feathers and spangles.

SPARKS—a shower *or* rain of sparks.

SPARROWS—a host, meinie *or* tribe of sparrows.

SPARS—a raffle of spars.

SPAWN—a fall of spawn.

SPEARS—a grove of spears; a plump of spearmen.

SPECIES—an aggregation of species.

SPECTATORS—an audience (*collectively*); a crowd *or* group of spectators.

SPEECHES—a deluge of buncombe.

SPICES—a seron (a bale *or* package of exotic spices)

SPIDERS—cluster *or* clutter of spiders.

SPIRES—a forest of spires.

SPIRITS—an exuberance *or* tumult of spirits.

SPOILS—a whack of spoils.

SQUALLS—a clutch of squalls.

SQUIRES—a squiry or squirarchy.

SQUIRRELS—a dray (*collectively*)

STABLES—a mews (a range of stables)

STAIRS—a flight of stairs, grece (stairs, *collectively*)

STAKES—a palisade of stairs.

STARLINGS—a cloud, a chattering *or* a murmuration of starlings.

STARS—a cluster; configuration, a conjuncture or constellation of stars; congeries of stars; a field, a galaxy, a knot of small stars; a multitude, a spangle *or* pleiad (a brilliant cluster) of stars.

STATES—an alliance, a coalition, a confederacy, a federation *or* a league of states.

STATESMEN—a disagreement of statesmen.

STATIONERY—a lot of stationery.

STATUES—a group of statues, *or* statuary (*collectively*)

STEEL—a blow of steel (a quantity of steel dealt with at one time in a converter); a burden *or* charge of steel; a garb (a bundle of steel rods)

STEPS—a flight of steps; a grece (steps *collectively*)

STEWARDS—a provision of stewards.

STICKLEBACKS—a shoal of sticklebacks.

STICKS—a bundle, fadge *or* faggot of sticks.

STOATS—a pack *or* trip of stoats.

STONES—a bourock (a stone heap or mound); a cairn, carol (ring), clatter (loose small stones) or confusion of stones; a cord (a measure); a huddle of large stones, a pile, raise *or* ruck of stones.

STORES (shops)—a chain of stores.

STORIES—a catch of stories; a posse of comic stories.

STORKS—a flight; a mustering of storks; a phalanx of migratory storks.

STORMS—a chain of storms.

STRANGERS—a band *or* rabble of strangers.

STRAWBERRIES—a mess of strawberries.

STRAW—a bolt, bottle, a bundle, a lock *or* tress of straw; a truss, a whisk *or* whisp (small bunch) of straw.

STREETS—a nest of alleys; a nest of quiet streets.

STRIKERS—a picket (*collectively*)

STUDENTS—a college of students; a conservatory of students; a dilation of pupils, *see also* ACADEMICS; PUPILS.

SUBJECTS (countrymen)—an army of subjects.

SUCCESSES—a confluence of successes.

SUGAR—a bag of sugar (75 kilos); a pot of sugar (originally 70 lb.)

SUNLIGHT—a beam, a pool *or* a shaft of sunlight.

SUPERSTITIONS—a bundle *or* a pack of superstitions.

SUSPECTS—a press of suspects.

SWALLOWS—a flight *or* a gulp of swallows.

SWANS—a bank, a bevy *or* an eyrar of swans; a drift, a game, a herd, a sownder, team *or* wedge of swans.

SWEARING, *see* OATHS.

SWIFTS—a flock of swifts.

SWINE—a doylt, a drove *or* a dryft of tame swine; a herd *or* trip of swine; a singular of boars; a sowner of wild swine.

SYCOPHANTS—a herd of sycophants.

TABLEWARE, *see* CUTLERY, DISHES.

TABLES—a nest of tables.

TAILORS—a disguising of tailors; a proud showing of tailors.

TALK—a knot *or* river of talk.

TAPSTERS—a promise of tapsters, *see also* INNKEEPERS.

TASTES—a hotch-potch of tastes.

TAVERNERS, *see* INNKEEPERS.

TAXIS—a fleet, a rank *or* a stand of taxis.

TEA—a break of tea (a large quantity); a lot *or* a consignment of tea.

TEACHERS—a conclave of teachers (a secret meeting); a school of teachers, *see also* ACADEMICS; KNOWLEDGE, PUPILS.

TEAL—a bunch, a coil, a diving, a knob, a leash (three) *or* a spring of teal.

TEARS—a flood, a river, a storm *or* a tribute of tears.

TEETH—a rage of teeth (aching teeth); an array of teeth; a case (or set) of teeth.

TELEGRAPH POLES—a forest of telegraph poles.

TEMPER, *see* ANGER.

TEMPESTS—a clutch of tempests.

TENANTS—tenantry (tenants, *collectively*)

TENEMENTS—a troop of tenements.

TENNIS PLAYERS—a set of tennis players.

TENTS—a camp (tents, *collectively*); canvas *or* tenting (*collectively*); a choir of tents.

TERRACES—a flight of terraces.

TERROR—fusillades of terror.

THIEVES—brigandage (*collectively*); a den, a family, a gang of thieves; a quest of cut-purses; a school *or* skulk of thieves, *see also* BANDITS, BRIGANDS, ROBBERS.

THINKERS—a breed of thinkers; a junto of wise men, *see also* KNOWLEDGE.

THORNS—a bush of thorns.

THOUGHT OR THOUGHTS—avenues of thought; a chain *or* host of thoughts; a mob of thoughts; a quest *or* train of thoughts; scatterings of thought; a well of serious thought.

THREAD—a lease, a knot *or* a clew of thread.

THREE—a harl, a leash, a tierce (third part); a triad, trio or trine (three things or people); triplets (three babies born at the same labour); triumvirate.

THRESHERS—a thrave of threshers.

THRUSHES—a mutation of thrushes.

THUNDER—a burst, a peal *or* a roll of thunder, *see also* STORMS, RAIN, SNOW.

TIMBER—a boom *or* raft of timber; a drive *or* sheaf of logs.

TIME—aeons (unmeasurable time); a cycle of years; a decade (ten years); a leash of days (three); oodles of time (plenty of time), *see also* YEARS.

TINKERS—a wandering of tinkers.

TINNERS—a convocation of tinners (Cornish)

TOADS—a knot of toads, a nest of toads; a chaplet of toads eggs.

TOASTS—a round of toasts.

TOBACCO—a bulk (a pile arranged for curing); a cake, a carrot, a wad of tobacco.

TOOLS—a bag *or* chest of tools.

TORTS—a tedium of torts (legal)

TOURISTS—a goggle of tourists.

TOW—a wad of tow (flax or hemp)

TRADING POSTS—a line of trading posts.

TRAFFIC—a congestion of traffic.

TRAITORS—a nest *or* sorte of traitors.

TRAMPS—monkery (*collectively*)

TRAPPERS—a brigade of trappers.

TRAVELLERS—a caravan (*collectively*); a fare of travellers (a company ready for travel)

TREASURE—a cache, mass, pose of treasure; treasure trove.

TREE SURGEONS—a graft of tree surgeons.

TREES—an avenue, a belt, a bouquet, a bosk, a bosket or bosquet of trees; a canopy, a clump, a forest; a frith (woods or wooded country, *collectively*); a grove, a group of trees; a knot of trees; a motte (clump on prairie); a palisade (trained in a row); a phalanx, a pile, a plantation, a plump (clump); a toft (small group); a faggot *or* whisk of twigs; a spray of branches, *see also* BRANCHES.

TRENCHES—a network of trenches.

TRICKS—a bag of tricks.

TRINKETS—trinketry (*collectively*)

TRIFLES—a truss of trifles.

TRIUMPHS—a series of triumphs.

TROOPS—an army; an array; a banner (body of men who follow a banner); battalion; battery; boast of soldiers; a bayonet of troops; a body of troops or soldiers; a brigade; cadre; cavalry (horse troops); chariotry (soldiers fighting from chariots); chiliarchy (a body of 1,000 troops); cohort of warriors; column of troops; comitadji (a band of irregulars); company; command; cordon; cornet of horse (a troop of cavalry); corps; a decade of troops (ten); a detachment of troops; a draft of troops (selected from other troops for some special duties); detail (troops put on special duties); echelon (drawn up in parallel lines); escort; file of troops; a force (*collectively*); formation of soldiers; garrison; generality (generals, *collectively*); a ging (a troop); a globe (drawn up in a circle); guard; a hosting (muster of armed men); legion (Roman unit of 3,000 to 6,000 troops); levy of troops; muster; orb (ring); parade; a parel of troops; patrol; phalanx of infantry; a picket; platoon; a power (body of armed men; range; rank; ray; regiment; rot (file of six soldiers); a rout; a rush of troops; a school; a sheltron (*Scottish*, band, squadron); squad; square; a shot of foot soldiers (with firearms); stand *or* troop of soldiers; troop of cavalry; troops (*collectively*); wedge; were, wered *or* wering (band of troops)

TROTTERS—a nest of trotters.

TROUBLES—basinful, heap *or* load of troubles; a peck, sea, shoal *or* whack of troubles.

TROUT—a brace (two); a hover (trout waiting on the edge of fast water); leash (three); a troup of trout.

TRUNKS—a host of trunks.

TUBES—tubing (*collectively*)

TUMULT—a congestion of tumult.

TUNES—a bunch *or* medley of tunes, *see* MUSIC.

TURF—a flaw (turf, *collectively*)

TURKEYS—a duet, a crop, posse of cock turkeys; a rafter of turkeys.

TURKS—a scourge of Turks.

TURNIPS—a camp (ridge-shaped heap)

TURRETS—an agglomeration, *see also* CASTLES.

TURTLES—a bale *or* turn of turtles.

TWELVE—a zodiac.

TWIGS—a cow, faggot, a tussock *or* whisk of twigs.

TWINE—a ball of twine.

TYPE (printing)—line of type; a pie (heap of type); a pillar of type (a column); a fount *or* font.

TYPISTS—a giggle or pool of typists.

ULCERS—a community of ulcers; a crop of ulcers.

UNDERGRADUATES & UNIVERSITIES—a consortium of universities; the faculty (the administration and teaching body); gown (collective term for the students of a college or university); an unemployment of graduates.

UNDERTAKERS—an unction of undertakers.

UNLAWFUL OR SECRET ACTS—a confederacy of unlawful acts.

URCHINS—a horde of urchins.

USHERS—a set of ushers.

UTTER IMPROBABILITIES—a faggot of utter improbabilities.

VAMPIRES—a colony of vampires.

VAPOURS—a bunch, a congregation, a pillar *or* a puff of vapours.

VARLETS—varletry (*collectively*)

VASSALS—vassalage (*collectively*)

VEINS—a network of veins.

VENDORS—a haggle of vendors.

VERSES—a cento of verses, *see also* Poems.

VESSELS (containers)—compages of vessels.

VESSELS, *see* Ships.

VICARS—a prudence of vicars; clergy *or* the cloth (*collectively*)

VICE—a den *or* torrent of vices; a commixture of virtues and vices.

VICTIMS—a covey of victims.

VICTUALS, *see* Food.

VILLAINS—a meinie of villains.

VINEGAR—a mess of vinegar.

VIOLINISTS—a string of violinists.

VIOLS—a consort *or* chest of viols.

VIPERS—a nest of vipers.

VIRGINS—a carol of virgins; a chapter of noble virgins; a consort of virgins; a college of handmaidens, *see also* GIRLS, LADIES, WOMEN.

VIRTUES—a catalogue of virtues; a commixture of virtues and vices; a dram of well doing; a fascicle of virtues.

VISITORS—a batch, a confusion *or* a flood of visitors.

VISITS—a round of visits.

VOCIFERATION—a concert of vociferation.

VOICES—a babel, concert, confluence *or* a medley of voices.

VOLCANIC FRAGMENTS—an agglomerate of volcanic fragments; a cascade of volcanic ash.

VOLCANOES—a rookery of volcanoes.

VOLES—a colony of voles.

VULTURES—a cast of vultures (two)

WAGGONS—a frame of waggons (a number travelling together); waggon park.

WAITERS—an army or an indifference of waiters, *see also* BUTLERS, RETAINERS, SERVANTS.

WALRUSES—a huddle of walruses.

WARRIORS—a breed *or* cohort of warriors, *see also* TROOPS.

WASPS—a bike, a nest *or* a swarm of wasps.

WATCHMEN—a pallor of nightwatchmen; the watch (*collectively*)

WATER—an accumulation of waters; a bolt (cylindrical jet), cascade *or* cataract of water; congeries of water particles; a debacle (a violent rush of water); a gush, a mass *or* a pat of water; a pillar, pocket *or* pool of water; reservoir; a rush, a spray *or* spurt of water.

WATERFOWL—a bunch of waterfowl.

WAX—a cake of wax.

WEALTH—an accumulation of wealth, *see also* MONEY.

WEAPONS—a pile *or* stack of weapons; an arsenal (*collectively*), *see also* GUNS AND GUNFIRE.

WEASELS—a pack of weasels.

WEDDING GUESTS—a convoy *or* party of wedding guests.

WEEPING—an outburst of weeping, *see also* TEARS.

WELL DOING—a dram of well doing.

WHALES—a gam; a grind (bottle-nosed whales); a herd of sperm whales; a mob, a plump, a pod, a run, *or* a school of whales.

WHALING SHIPS—a gam of whaling ships.

WHARVES—a nest of wharves; wharfage *or* wharfing (*collectively*)

WHEAT, *see* CORN.

WHELPS—legions of whelps.

WHITING—a pod of whiting.

WICKED MEN—a covin of wicked men.

WIDGEON—a bunch of widgeon (in water); a company; a flight of widgeon (in the air); a knob of widgeon (in the water)

WIDOWS—an ambush of widows.

WILD CATS—a destruction *or* a dout of wild cats.

WILD PIGS—a sounder, a drift *or* a singular of wild pigs.

WILDFOWL—a lute, a plump, a scry, a skein, a sord *or* a trip of wildfowl.

WIND—a capful of wind; a congregation of winds; a flurry, a gust, a puff, a rack (sudden rush), a rush *or* a sailful of wind.

WINE—a cellar (wine, *collectively*); a congery of wine; a dozen (12 bottles)

WING COMMANDERS—a flush of wing commanders.

WISE MEN—a junto *or* a resort of wise men.

WISHES—a brood of guilty wishes; a farrago of wishes.

WIT—a breed of wits (humorists); a junto of wits; a smack of wit; a treasury of wit.

WITCHES—a cloud, a coven, a covin, a convent, a knot *or* a pack of witches.

WITNESSES—a cloud *or* an orb of witnesses.

WIVES—a harem (*collectively*); a nonpatience *or* an impatience of wives.

WOES—a cluster, a field, a group, a load *or* a parcel of woes.

WOLVES—a head of hungry wolves; a horde, a pack, a rout *or* a route of wolves.

WOMEN—a bevy of women; a gaggle; a posse of silly women; womenhood (*collectively*); the monstrous regiment of women, *see also* GIRLS, LADIES, PROSTITUTES, VIRGINS.

WOOD—a bavin (bundle of brushwood); a cord, dram or faggot of wood; a fascine of wood (long bundle of wood bound together); a fathom *or* knitch of wood; a pile, a stack *or* a whisk (twigs) of wood, *see also* TIMBER.

WOODCOCK—a fall, a covey *or* a flight of woodcock.

WOODPECKERS—a descent of woodpeckers.

WOOL—a pad, a skein of wool.

WORDS—an army *or* century of words; a flood of fiery words; groups of words; a conglomeration of words; a jumble, a rabble, a rhapsody *or* a riot of words; a rout, a stream or a scaffolding of words; a thesaurus, a torrent, a train *or* a volley of words; verbiage (too many words)

WORK—jobbery.

WORKMEN—a factory (originally a body of factors or workmen); a gang of workmen; a darg (a specific quantity of work)

WORMS—a bed *or* a clew of worms.

WORRIES, *see* TROUBLES.

WORSHIPPERS—a congregation of worshippers; a chapelry.

WRATH—accumulation of wrath, a sea *or* storm of wrath, *see also* ANGER.

WRENS—a herd of wrens.

WRESTLERS—a crunch of wrestlers.

WRINKLES—a network of wrinkles.

WRITERS—a pleiad (a brilliant group of writers); a sect or a worship of writers, *see also* AUTHORS.

WRITINGS—a corpus of writings.

WRY FACES—a parcel of wry faces.

YACHTS—a plump of yachts.

YARN—a clew, a cycle, a decade, a knot, a lea *or* a pad of yarn.

YEARS—a power of years; pentad (five years); a cycle of years; a decade, *see also* TIME.

YEOMEN—a fellowship of yeomen; yeomenry (*collectively*)

YOUNG READERS—a horde of young readers.

YOUTHS—a crop of beardless youths.

ZEBRAS—a zeal of zebras.